GOD'S
RULES FOR
HOLINESS

GOD'S
RULES FOR
HOLINESS

PETER MASTERS

THE WAKEMAN TRUST * LONDON

GOD'S RULES FOR HOLINESS

© Peter Masters 2003

THE WAKEMAN TRUST
(UK Registered Charity)

Website: www.wakemantrust.org

UK Registered Office
38 Walcot Square
London SE11 4TZ

US Office
300 Artino Drive
Oberlin, OH 44074-1263

ISBN 1 870855 37 X

Cover design by Andrew Owen

Printed by Stephens & George, Merthyr Tydfil, UK

CONTENTS

Prologue: Five Crucial Keys   9

1   Putting God First   21

2   Making God Small   33

3   Keeping Close to the Lord   39

4   The Believer's Special Day   49

5   God's Plan for His Church   59

6   Murderers All!   69

7   One Fence to Disaster   83

8   The Many Faces of Theft   97

9   A Family of Lies   109

10   Enemy of the Heart   123

Epilogue: The 'Secret' of Blessing   137

Appendix: The Abiding Authority of the Commandments   141

AND GOD SPAKE ALL THESE WORDS, SAYING, I AM THE LORD THY GOD, WHICH HAVE BROUGHT THEE OUT OF THE LAND OF EGYPT, OUT OF THE HOUSE OF BONDAGE.

1   THOU SHALT HAVE NO OTHER GODS BEFORE ME.

2   THOU SHALT NOT MAKE UNTO THEE ANY GRAVEN IMAGE, OR ANY LIKENESS OF ANY THING THAT IS IN HEAVEN ABOVE, OR THAT IS IN THE EARTH BENEATH, OR THAT IS IN THE WATER UNDER THE EARTH: THOU SHALT NOT BOW DOWN THYSELF TO THEM, NOR SERVE THEM . . .

3   THOU SHALT NOT TAKE THE NAME OF THE LORD THY GOD IN VAIN; FOR THE LORD WILL NOT HOLD HIM GUILTLESS THAT TAKETH HIS NAME IN VAIN.

4   REMEMBER THE SABBATH DAY, TO KEEP IT HOLY. SIX DAYS SHALT THOU LABOUR, AND DO ALL THY WORK: BUT THE SEVENTH DAY IS THE SABBATH OF THE LORD THY GOD: IN IT THOU SHALT NOT DO ANY WORK . . . FOR IN SIX DAYS THE LORD MADE HEAVEN AND EARTH, THE SEA, AND ALL THAT IN THEM IS, AND RESTED THE SEVENTH DAY: WHEREFORE THE LORD BLESSED THE SABBATH DAY, AND HALLOWED IT.

5   HONOUR THY FATHER AND THY MOTHER: THAT THY DAYS MAY BE LONG UPON THE LAND WHICH THE LORD THY GOD GIVETH THEE.

6   THOU SHALT NOT KILL.

7   THOU SHALT NOT COMMIT ADULTERY.

8   THOU SHALT NOT STEAL.

9   THOU SHALT NOT BEAR FALSE WITNESS AGAINST THY NEIGH-BOUR.

10   THOU SHALT NOT COVET THY NEIGHBOUR'S HOUSE, THOU SHALT NOT COVET THY NEIGHBOUR'S WIFE, NOR HIS MAN-SERVANT, NOR HIS MAIDSERVANT, NOR HIS OX, NOR HIS ASS, NOR ANY THING THAT IS THY NEIGHBOUR'S.

EXODUS 20.1-17, KING JAMES VERSION

'Written with the finger of God.' *(Exodus 31.18)*

Five Crucial Keys

'The law is holy, and the commandment
holy, and just, and good.'
(Romans 7.12)

IN A GRAND but dilapidated mansion run as a Christian conference centre, a small group of people were talking in a lounge, and somehow the subject turned to the Ten Commandments. A student, speaking cautiously as if not wanting to offend, said he didn't find the Commandments very challenging or useful for personal sanctification, because they dealt mainly with extreme sins like idolatry, adultery, stealing and murder. He acknowledged that they mentioned the Sabbath and lying, but still puzzled over the lack of rules on pride or selfishness or bad temper, not to mention many other sins he struggled with.

An older man in the room said the Commandments were probably not specific enough, and he could understand how the rich young ruler could imagine he had kept them all. A young woman felt they were too negative, whereas she wanted positive advice on how she should live, such as that in the Beatitudes of the Sermon on the Mount, or Paul's fruit of the Spirit: love, joy, peace, longsuffering, and so on. These were surely more relevant for Christians.

All these people were earnest Christians who would never have meant to disparage any part of the Bible. A pastor in the group then embarked on a defence of the Commandments, pointing out that they were the source and summary of every other passage in the Bible about holy living, covering every conceivable sin – including pride and anger. He outlined their role, scope, and positive features, showing how perfectly they serve modern Christians in the quest for holiness and character.

The writer of this book was not that pastor, but what follows in the next few pages is the kind of response he may well have given – in more developed form. It will set out briefly five facts it is vital to know about the Commandments if their full scope and depth is to be seen. In summary the five keys for unlocking the Commandments are these:–

Firstly, *they reflect God's character.* What a motive this is to respect and study them!

Secondly, *they keep their full authority today.* It is so important to know that they tower above the old ceremonial and civic laws given temporarily to the children of Israel.

Thirdly, *they were designed for believers.* Certainly, they are binding on all mankind, but when their full contents are recognised, they are especially relevant to Christian people, even providing rules for worship and for the structure of the church.

Fourthly – and this key has a dramatic effect on how we apply the Commandments – *each one covers a whole family of sins.*

Fifthly, these Commandments, though mainly expressed in negative form, are also *commands to perform the opposite positive virtues.*

The last two keys particularly revolutionise our use of this mighty code for holiness.

There is nothing quite like these Commandments for stimulating progress in sanctification, once our minds are primed to see all that they teach. In the New Testament we read that keeping them is an act of love to Christ *(John 14.15)*, and also the basis of assurance *(1 John 3.18-19)*. It is true that keeping them cannot save a single soul, but for believers, saved by grace through faith in Christ alone, they are priceless. This book will follow the five biblical keys as its method of unlocking the riches of the 'royal law'.

1. The Commandments Reflect God's Character

First, it is essential to realise that the Ten Commandments flow directly from the eternal character of the holy God, and reflect Him. We must not regard them as an inferior, early version of God's law; a primitive code designed only for the time of the Old Testament. They have been wrongly called temporary regulations framed to keep the human race in order while living in a fallen world, but they are far more than this. It is because they reflect God's perfect character that they are the standard by which the world will be judged, and also the permanent rule of life for redeemed people.

Even the great nineteenth-century American theologian Charles Hodge loses sight of this vital fact when he says that the commandments about murder, marriage and property will cease to have relevance beyond this present life, and are therefore 'not founded on the essential nature of God'. This view is out of line with the traditional mainstream of Bible commentators, and severely limits the personal application of these commandments. Once we grasp that all the Commandments reflect God's own holy character, then we see that our innermost nature must be shaped by them.

We see, for example, that the sixth commandment condemns murder because it is the unchanging character of God to preserve and to deal very kindly with His people. The Lord will Himself keep the sixth commandment for ever in the eternal glory, where none of His people will ever perish. It is the character of God not to hurt or destroy anyone, aside from the just punishment of sin. Moses (as we shall see) links the sin of murder with that of taking away another person's liberty, and with destroying the dignity of ageing parents. Whenever people are despised or emotionally crushed, something similar to murder is committed. The chief reason why this is evil is that it is contrary to the character of God, Who is love. We are to become more like Him in lovingkindness – an application which is obvious when we discern that each commandment is based on the character of our glorious God.

Similarly, the seventh commandment reflects the *faithfulness* of God. The ban on adultery is not merely an expedient to regulate human sexual behaviour in this present evil world. It is a commandment which will be perfectly kept (in the highest sense) throughout all eternity by God and His redeemed people, for they will be utterly loyal to one another. Once we see that this commandment flows from the character of God, we see that its scope extends far beyond marriage, and we are not surprised when Isaiah, Jeremiah, Paul and James (among other inspired writers) all use this commandment to teach the duty of *spiritual* loyalty.

The eighth commandment – 'Thou shalt not steal' – also reflects the wonderful character of the Lord, Who is the great giver and not the spoiler of men. His blessings are countless and free, and His people are to resemble Him by being those who give out, not those who sponge, or feed upon, or who drain away the resources (and emotional strength) of others. The eighth commandment goes well beyond the act of physical theft. (Tragically, many Christians who have never stolen anything material are passengers and burdens in their churches, and therefore are thieves, contributing nothing by way of spiritual witness or effort.) The eighth commandment rests on God's infinitely benevolent character.

These examples provide just a glimpse of the full pastoral application that springs to view as soon as we see the Commandments as an expression of the character and tastes of Almighty God. But how can we be so sure that they reflect the character of God? The answer is that God has said so, for when He commanded Moses to proclaim the moral law to the people He began with these words: 'Ye shall be holy: for I the Lord your God am holy' *(Leviticus 19.2)*.

Similar statements occur several times in the books of Moses, all indicating that the moral law was given as an extension of the character of God, or a description of His holiness. The apostle Paul also teaches that the Commandments are more than rules imposed by God for the regulation of society, repeatedly emphasising that they are *spiritual* in character. In *Romans 7.12* and *14* he says – 'Wherefore the law is holy, and the commandment holy, and just, and good . . . the law is spiritual.' We must be clear, therefore, that the moral code of the Ten Commandments reveals God's wonderful nature and divine attributes.

2. The Commandments Keep Their Full Authority Today

The second key for unlocking the riches of the Commandments is to know that they are God's perpetual rules for worship and holy living. This point naturally follows from the first. After all, if the Commandments reflect the unchanging character of God, it follows they will be supreme over any changing arrangements from the Old Testament era to the New. People often ask why the Ten Commandments should be separated from the civil and ceremonial laws which God gave to Moses, and regarded as the supreme expression of

God's moral law. Why should those other laws be swept away while the Ten Commandments keep their authority?

The answer may be given easily enough from the New Testament, where we find all the Ten Commandments affirmed in the teaching of Christ and His apostles. Some teachers say that the fourth commandment, about the Sabbath or Lord's Day, is the exception, but they are mistaken, as we shall show in the study of that commandment.

The special status of the Ten Commandments is especially stated by Moses, who draws attention to the way in which they were delivered, saying: 'These words the Lord spake unto all your assembly in the mount out of the midst of the fire, of the cloud, and of the thick darkness, with a great voice: and he added no more. And he wrote them in two tables of stone, and delivered them unto me' *(Deuteronomy 5.22). Exodus 31.18* adds that the Commandments were 'written with the finger of God'.

God chose a unique way of communicating this particular portion of His Word. Generally He spoke through inspired human messengers – prophets and apostles – but He delivered these Commandments by a mighty voice from Heaven and wrote them in stone with His own 'finger'. This direct manner of communication lifted the Ten Commandments high above the ceremonial and civic laws which followed. They were dramatically marked out as different, and 'elevated' to a position from which they would ever shine across both testaments.

Immediately after the giving of the Ten Commandments, the Lord revealed a host of other requirements to the Israelites in a less spectacular way, through Moses. He gave more detailed explanations of the Commandments, added many laws for specific situations, and also appended the religious ceremonial laws. These secondary laws were designed for the following purposes:

(1) to educate the minds of the people to understand vital

concepts such as the holiness of God and the need for mediation and sacrifice;

(2) to provide a temporary system of worship until Christ came;

(3) to be visual aids pointing forward to the work of the Messiah.

All these secondary laws, both civic and ceremonial, were intended to operate only until Christ came, although their underlying principles have many lessons and applications for today. Nevertheless, the Ten Commandments stand above them all as the abiding moral law of God, and we must discount any teaching which places them on the same level as the laws which were terminated by the coming of Christ.

3. The Commandments Were Designed for Believers

The third key to seeing the riches of the Ten Commandments is the realisation that they were given to serve a two-fold purpose. They were obviously intended to be binding upon all mankind, yet at the same time they were designed to be particularly helpful to those who truly know and love the Lord. For mankind generally the Ten Commandments are the standards of righteousness for acceptance with God, barring the approach to Heaven to guilty and unforgiven people. Sinners can only be washed and redeemed because Christ has fulfilled the law's demands on their behalf, and paid the eternal punishment of sin for His people.

Before conversion, the Commandments tower over us to condemn and convict, but once we have been brought to Christ, the same Commandments wear a friendly smile and become a great guide and help. On the one hand they are absolutely binding upon the whole human race as the basis of judgement, and on the other they are the manual of conduct, worship and blessing for all saved people. We learn this from Moses, who emphasises the special suitability of the law for believers in these words: 'And thou shalt love the Lord thy God with all thine heart, and with all thy soul, and with all thy might. And these words, which I command thee this day, shall be in thine heart' *(Deuteronomy 6.5-6)*. Moses did not here speak of an obedience of fear, but introduced the law as something designed to be a blessing to those who love the Lord. For them, the Commandments would be directive, and also precious, compelling and inspiring.

Do we find such inspiration in the Commandments? We may if we hold this key, namely, the realisation that they were largely framed with born-again people in view. When the Lord introduced the Commandments to the people, He said, 'I am the Lord thy God, which have brought thee out of the land of Egypt, out of the house of bondage.' These words show their special relevance to people who had found liberty and deliverance from God. They were written as a code of kindness, the 'formula' for continuing in liberty. God's purpose was to protect His dear children from harm, and so He said (in effect), 'I have brought you from bondage to liberty, and here are the rules which will keep you in the way of blessing.'

The dual function of the Commandments is like a great iron drawbridge barring the way to a castle surrounded by a wide moat. Once raised, it is impossible to break down the drawbridge, but should the signal be given to let someone into the castle, that impassable barrier swings down to bridge the moat. Once lowered, the person entering sees a solid iron road with strong, safe handrails, and the menacing barrier becomes a help and a support. This illustration falls short of the mark because the Ten Commandments are in no sense a bridge or mediator between man and God, nevertheless, salvation transforms the Commandments from enemies to friends. We must therefore approach the Commandments with a high expectation of personal, pastoral help and counsel. We must expect to hear from them a kindly, protective word. One of them, for example, when seen in this light, is a commandment to protect churches against the instability of inexperienced leadership. How can we be guaranteed as Christians the wonderful blessings of God, including clear evidence of His presence? The answer is – by these Commandments. Though they are binding upon all men, and though they certainly include stern prohibitions, they are among God's kindest and most productive words for the protection and refining of believers.

4. Each Commandment Covers a 'Family' of Sins

The fourth key to unlocking the full value of the Commandments is indispensable, for, when this key is neglected, any exposition or understanding becomes superficial in the extreme. This fourth key is the belief that each sin named in the Commandments represents an entire species of sin. Each sin named is the chief offence of a whole family of wrong deeds. Moses demonstrates this principle in several passages, and the New Testament confirms it repeatedly. It is well known, for example, that the commandment against adultery also covers lust in the heart, and the commandment against murder includes hatred. Therefore when a commandment forbids a major sin, all the 'lesser' sins in the same family are to be included in the scope of that commandment.

The Commandments are certainly to be taken at face value, and obeyed at the level of the sin named, but to limit the Commandments to the sins specifically mentioned robs them of all but their surface meaning. We must always ask – What other sins are in the same family as the chief and representative offence named? Moses frequently provides the answer for us as he explains the law further, and we shall refer to his 'commentary' in the following chapters. When, for example, idols and images are forbidden, we realise that this is the chief sin of a family, and non-literal forms of idol are included. If, therefore, there is something in our worship or in our lives which becomes a source of carnal enjoyment or satisfaction, displacing God, then it is an idol. Similarly, literal adultery is the worst sin in a family of offences that includes all other forms of unfaithfulness, and also *spiritual* adultery. We shall explore (and prove) these 'families' of sin in the chapters ahead.

5. The Commandments Include Opposite Positive Virtues

The final key for understanding and appreciating the Commandments is the conviction that they are meant to be handled in a positive, as well as a negative, manner. While couched in negative tones, God means us to strive for the opposite virtue of every sin. The Commandments are expressed in a negative way because their first function is to highlight man's sinfulness, but believers are to love and pursue the opposite qualities of each forbidden thing. This is how the New Testament teaches us to view the Commandments, as, for example, in *Hebrews 13.5*, where we read – 'Let your conversation be without covetousness; and be content with such things as ye have: for he hath said, I will never leave thee, nor forsake thee.' Contentment and reliance on the Lord are the positive virtues derived from the tenth commandment.

This was a method of interpretation which God intended His people to adopt from the very beginning, Moses being inspired to set the example when he says, 'And thou shalt love the Lord thy God with all thine heart, and with all thy soul, and with all thy might' *(Deuteronomy 6.5),* words later chosen by the Lord Jesus as a perfect summary of the first table of the Commandments. It was always intended that true believers should see the positive side of each prohibition. Moses again calls us to think about the positive virtues, saying, 'Ye shall diligently keep the commandments of the Lord your God, and his testimonies, and his statutes, which he hath commanded thee. And thou shalt do that which is right and good in the sight of the Lord: that it may be well with thee' *(Deuteronomy 6.17-18)*. Nothing could be more positive than this fatherly exhortation. If we fail to identify the good behaviour implicit in each commandment we miss the point entirely. We must from each one build up a solid appreciation of the kind of people that God wants us to be, noting the contrasting good deed of each sin.

* * * * *

Before we embark on this study, it should be made clear that we depend on Christ alone for all our blessing, throughout life. Believers do not earn or secure their continuing blessing by obedience to the law, for all benefits, lifelong, come solely through the merits and work of Christ. Our striving for holiness cannot earn anything, for we fall so far short of God's righteousness. Nevertheless, God requires that we should willingly, gladly desire to walk by the moral law, to please and honour Him. A small child may receive a reward for good behaviour, perhaps an outing or a gift, but the child's efforts do not earn the money to pay for the reward. Similarly, God 'rewards' the righteous, but these rewards are entirely purchased by our Lord and Saviour Jesus Christ, and are rewards of grace. Indifference to God's Commandments, however, will forfeit much spiritual comfort, assurance, instrumentality and answered prayer, and may even bring the Lord's hand of discipline upon us (see *Hebrews 12*).

Scripture verses confirming the abiding authority of
the Commandments are provided in an appendix, page 141.

1

The First Commandment
'Thou shalt have no other gods before me.'

Putting God First

'. . . that in all things he
might have the preeminence.'
(Colossians 1.18)

THE FIRST COMMANDMENT anticipates all the mercy and promises of the Gospel, telling us that we may know God and relate to Him. It assures us that it is possible for us to come near to Him, worship Him, glory in Him and draw all our needs from Him. It is a truly momentous statement by God about His availability to every trusting soul, for this commandment in effect says, 'I will be good and gracious to you; I will be approachable by you; I will be a Father, Saviour and Friend to you, and you will need no other gods beside Me. You may come to Me, love Me, prove My presence, and receive My forgiveness, life and power. You may share in My eternal purposes, and be My child, and I will be your God for ever.'

All this is the logical conclusion to be drawn from the fact that we shall need no other god beside the Lord. Because we may know the infallible and glorious Lord of all, there is no reason or excuse for us to turn to other gods, whether of a religious or secular kind. With such access to Him, God insists that we make *Him* our only object of worship, recognise Him as the sole source of life and truth, and yield to His lordship.

Defining Other Gods

What are these 'other gods' referred to in this commandment? Clearly they are not just pagan idols. To have 'other gods' is defined by Matthew Henry in these words:–

> 'To love, to desire, to delight in, or to expect any good from any sinful indulgence, is prohibited. Equally, we are not to allow any person or created thing, however valuable or excellent, to rival God in our affections. All atheism, infidelity and irreligion is opposition to God, an attempt to be independent of Him. The proud man is his own idol because he worships himself and expects others to do the same. The covetous man makes a god of his wealth, which he loves, depends upon and expects happiness from. The sensualist by his practices worships "deities" as filthy as any seen in a pagan temple.'

Does the Bible intend us to extend the meaning of 'other gods' in this way? Is this the original, literal sense of the first commandment? It certainly is, because the deities of the ancient world stood for, and encouraged, the seeking of gratification in creature things and in self. The first commandment was intended to forbid not only pagan gods, but *all that they represented.*

Before conversion, the idol of 'self' is often, if not usually, our supreme God. Pride reigns, in all its forms, so that *we* take the first place in our lives. We worship and serve 'number one', and our selfish objectives blot out all interest in the true God. After conversion, pride and self-love become our greatest enemies as we see them as 'idols' rivalling the Lord Who has saved us.

Idolatry is the worship of (or reliance on) anything *in the place of God*, including ourselves, and embraces all idols whether they are intellectual idols, emotional idols, material idols or sensual idols. The New Testament shows us that we must interpret the first commandment in this way. In *Colossians 3.5*, for example, Paul lists the sins of immorality, unclean thoughts, lust, evil desire and covetousness, and immediately says such conduct is – *idolatry*. No literal pagan god is involved, but to seek all our gratification from earthly things is a form of idol worship.

Paul says the same in *Ephesians 5.5* – 'For this ye know, that no whoremonger, nor unclean person, nor covetous man, who is an idolater, hath any inheritance in the kingdom of Christ and of God.' Paul also shows that greed may be a breach of the first commandment, for in *Philippians 3.19* he speaks of certain false teachers 'whose God is their belly . . . who mind earthly things'. In the language of the Bible, all uncontrolled appetites become gods.

No Other Gods At All

To discover the full sense of the commandment it is necessary to explain the last two words: 'Thou shalt have no other gods – *before me.*' It is possible for us to misread these words to mean – 'you may have no other god in front of me, ahead of me, or above me.' This reading would enable us to have many idols in our lives, so long as they did not challenge the supreme place we give to God, and it is exactly this compromise that Satan wants to bring about in us. However, the words 'before me' do not mean 'ahead of me', but – 'in my sight' (which is exactly how William Tyndale translated it in his New Testament of 1530). It is a forceful way of saying, 'Thou shalt have no other gods at all!'

It is obvious that we should not support any god which is *against* the Lord. But what about a god which claims to be on the same side as Him? Some Christians, for example, try to justify their worldly fashions, music, and pursuit of wealth on the ground that all these things will be dedicated to the Lord's work. Their expensive fashion clothes will help worldlings to feel comfortable in their presence. Their rock music will be employed to attract crowds to church. Their luxurious homes filled with fabulous creature comforts will be used for evangelistic house-group meetings. The gods of extreme self-indulgence can (they think) be adapted, tamed and sanitised for use on 'the Lord's side'. Some professing Bible-Christians seem to think that even false religion can be sanctified, so they link up in ecumenical ventures with Catholics and Bible-denying 'liberals'. However, the first commandment condemns all other gods, religious or material, regardless of whether they are antagonistic to the true God or adapted for use on His side.

The greatest recurring problem of the Israelites in Old Testament times was that they worshipped the Lord and other gods *at the same time.* God's comment upon the people is found in *2 Kings 17.41* – 'So these nations feared the Lord, and served their graven images.' God says in the first commandment, 'You shall not put your affection and reliance on anything to replace Me, or to assist Me, as though I had no power.'

Unexpected Gods

This first, deeply challenging commandment searches our motives, and in the remainder of this chapter we must allow it to speak to us. As unbelievers we once filled our lives with all manner of things which served as *alternatives* to God. We did not want to seek the Lord and find Him, so the void within us had to be filled with various pleasures, entertainments, business interests, ambitions, and

pursuit of possessions. It is true that some pleasures and possessions, kept in proportion, are clean, worthy and legitimate, but are
some of these things still our gods? Our first definition of 'other
gods' must run along these lines:

> Anything which I choose to do which is a real diversion, distrac-
> tion or alternative to my worship of the Lord, is effectively
> 'another god'. Similarly, anything which spoils or impairs my
> wholehearted service to the Lord is 'another god'.

Alternatives to God come in many shapes, one common form
being day-dreams which bring us happiness and satisfaction by
focusing on materialistic or selfish desires. The roving imagination
can become home to many a mental idol, and so we need to challenge ourselves from time to time asking, 'What have I been
dreaming about through this past week?' We must not allow our
minds to become lodging places to an endless procession of passing
gods.

Some believers suffer from addiction to anxiety, fretting and constant worry about trivial, domestic arrangements so that their minds
are unavailable to the living God and the major things of life.
Whether we realise it or not, if we allow plans and problems to
become a serious distraction they assume the status of 'other gods'
because they rob God of our emotional energy for reflection, prayer
and service and therefore take His place. Sometimes, when the time
for prayer draws near, almost any other matter can suddenly seem
much more interesting or more important or more pressing than
prayer. Whatever steals the place of God in that precious and privileged appointment with Him virtually becomes a god.

Here is another way of defining 'other gods': anyone or anything
to which I give undue or supreme admiration and affection is
another god. We can admire many people and many things in this
world, holding them in affection and esteem, but when a person or
thing begins to occupy a *dominating place* in our affections it is

probably becoming a god. Special care is needed in identifying such a god because God has given us a great capacity to love, appreciate and enjoy things. It is entirely legitimate to be fascinated by all manner of things around us. We even have a commission from the Word to explore, subdue, understand and enjoy the universe in which God has set us. However, it is our responsibility to ensure that our interest in these things never challenges our obedience and commitment to the Lord.

Antidotes to Other Gods

Detailed advice on this point is given under the tenth commandment, but here are two remedies or antidotes to restrain the emergence of 'other gods' in our life. The first helps to counteract any unduly strong feelings of attachment or excitement in connection with material or earthly things. Instead of allowing our powers of appreciation and enjoyment complete liberty to dwell on our possessions, careers, businesses, children, homes, clothes, hobbies and so on, we should rein in those powers whenever the object is *something for me*. If it is *my* possession, *my* career, or *my* appearance (which I am shopping for or thinking about), I must try to take a sober and low-key interest in the matter. I must determine not to get excited about such things, but to be more matter-of-fact about them, and I must set for myself relatively basic and reasonable standards. By adopting this policy we shall curb the tendency to worship worldly things at the point where they get their greatest hold over us – the point where they serve our pride and self-love. So we say, 'If it is something for me which is in mind, I shall refuse to get carried away and day-dream about it. I propose to be simple and straightforward in my personal requirements. I shall not spend days planning the decor, or revelling in various plans. If it is a *personal* matter, I shall keep a tight control on myself.'

This does not mean that we dress in sackcloth and live in dilapidated houses, but that we designate *personal* plans, pursuits and possessions as a potentially dangerous area. Anything falling into this category will be regarded with a degree of coolness, and we shall take steps to curtail any tendency to over-admire, or revel in this kind of thing. Instead, our capacity for appreciation and enjoyment will be invested in the work of God, and we will become much more interested in its successes and needs. Let us put the best of our ability to dream and plan into the work of the Lord's kingdom. By all means let the faculty for appreciation and enjoyment be allowed to run more freely when the object is connected with the Lord's work, or with the circumstances of *other* people. The Word commands us to love one another, to – 'Look not every man on his own things, but every man also on the things of others' (see *Philippians 2.3-7*). So, when my capacity for planning, and my interests are aroused over some scheme or object, it is good to ask, 'Is it for me? Is it mine?' If so, let the alarm bells sound because another god is about to be nurtured in the soul. But if the scheme or object is for someone else, or an employer, or best of all for the Lord, I am on safer ground.

Another method which should be used to dissolve strong feelings of attachment to some earthly thing is to give the faculty of appreciation more exercise in the area of *natural things*. We live in an unnatural age, life being cluttered with human technology and manufactured things. In the cities we seldom see the stars, the hills – the skies and landscapes which helped keep the psalmists enraptured by a worthy view of God. When we get the opportunity to go out and look at beautiful views – created things which are all to the immediate credit of the Lord – then, again, we are on safer ground for our powers of appreciation and delight. In summary, therefore, the areas of natural things, our service to others, and chiefly, our service for the Gospel, are the best places to put to work our powers of imagination, for in these areas we shall be much less likely to make 'other gods' out of things. The greatest danger is always when something is 'for me'. We have a solemn responsibility for self-control and balance, and if we fail in this we shall find ourselves serving other gods. We are commanded – 'Set your affection on things above, not on things on the earth.'

Discerning the Gods in Our Lives

1. Could we do without it?

The question arises – How do I know if I love or depend upon something so much that it has become another god? How can I tell when I have become too attached to something or someone? The answer comes, first, in the form of another question: 'Would I be prepared to do without that item or that person, however close, if the Lord required this of me?' Take the situation often faced by persecuted Christians. They know that if they continue with their worship, preaching and youth evangelism they may have to suffer imprisonment and family separation for years. For married couples and families the prospect seems intolerable, for God has called them to love each other and to maintain the closest possible bond. Nevertheless, they believe that the Lord must come first. When the day comes that we would not be prepared to suffer loss – not even for a while – then even the holy love of Christian marriage will have become 'another god'. Marriage is the gift of God, the very expression of His own love, and yet it can become a tainted thing if it comes before the Lord and our faithfulness to Him. Precious as such relationships are, we are given them so that we may dedicate them to the service of the Lord. God gives us wonderful blessings in friendships and in marriage, but He must always come first. In lands of freedom we are not called upon to forfeit the benefits of being together in order to serve the Lord, yet some Christian couples even protest at the minor trial of being separated for an evening of Christian service, such as visitation. The question is – Does the Lord and His service always come first?

2. Has it begun to rule us?

Another indication that something has become another god is when some activity, possession, or relationship has come to rule us. 'All things are lawful unto me,' says Paul, 'but all things are not expedient: all things are lawful for me, but I will not be brought under the power of any' *(1 Corinthians 6.12)*. Some people are ruled by their relations or friends. Obviously we must maintain a good testimony before our unconverted relations, but it is sad to see Christian people allowing themselves to be manipulated, dominated and intimidated by ungodly parents or relatives. Younger believers sometimes accept substantial financial and other help from unbelieving relations and then find themselves in the grip of a moral debt, so that they are at their beck and call for years. For such believers, their family has become a god to be looked to for help, and then a god that must be obeyed.

Tragically, some believers make a god of their careers and study courses and thus lose control of doing everything for the Lord. Careful balance is needed in these matters, because study and advance is wholesome, but some allow themselves to be ruled and overwhelmed by these pursuits so that they can never take their place serving the Lord in their local church. Their supreme objective is to be really significant people earning the highest possible salaries, but what if the Lord has other plans for such students? This is too bad because everything is already worked out and the situation is not open to discussion. Certain goals have become gods, and the true God must not intervene.

We accept that God may call some of His children to go to the very top in various professions. He alone is the General in charge of His army. But His Word also says – 'Seekest thou great things for thyself? seek them not' – and it is wrong for believers to pursue relentlessly worldly goals in abject surrender to the world's value system, which makes a god of higher education and personal advancement.

3. Does it stir us to urgency?

Another way of telling whether we have other gods in our lives is to notice those things that most stir our sense of responsibility and urgency. We rightly take many things seriously, responding imme-diately to emergencies in both family and business life, but do we feel or react in the same way for God's affairs? Pastors often com-plain that there are church officers who seem to lack any concern, let alone urgency, about the problems and hurts of the work of God. Endeavours can go wrong and need attention; people may be in need of transportation or care; departments may run down – yet throughout all these problems some officers remain supremely relaxed and untroubled. Their domestic and personal trials are per-haps the *only* matters of real importance to them. Is this so with us? Going beyond church officers, how many church members notice and respond to local church 'emergencies'? This is an effective pointer to the gods in our lives – those things which most readily stir feelings of anxiety and concern. Obviously it is right to react in a responsible and urgent way to family and business emergencies, but if we do not give at least equal attention to the Lord's affairs then we make family and business gods.

4. Is it for me, or for the Lord?

Finally, *our motives betray our gods.* Is my goal or motive to be noticed and admired? Is it to be comfortable and happy? If so, that goal is a god, loved, needed and served by us. If we are Sunday

School teachers and our ultimate goal is to be *seen* to have a big class (or at least a larger class than anyone else) then *prestige* has become a god. As a preacher, do I desire numerical results so that others will admire a large congregation? If this is my interest and goal, then pride and self-esteem have become my god. If, on the other hand, my objective is to do all I can for the Lord, for the winning of souls, and for His eternal glory, then the Lord is my Master and God.

Do we want people to regard us as clever, witty, strong, spiritual, eloquent, knowledgeable, or anything else? What drives us in all our activities? We must ask ourselves – 'What is my motive? Why do I serve the Lord? What is my objective? Is it a self-vaunting one, or do I act to serve the Lord because I love Him?' We have to think about these issues because God has said we must never finally rely on, be ruled by, or have supreme affection for anything other than Himself. We need to exercise great thoughtfulness if we are to obey the first commandment – 'Thou shalt have no other gods before me.' Our prayer must be, 'Lord, help me to purge my heart, and to seek all my good in Thee. Enable me to recognise my fault should other things take over my life.'

2

The Second Commandment
'Thou shalt not make . . . any graven image.'

Making God Small

'O the depth of the riches both of the
wisdom and knowledge of God! how unsearchable
are his judgments, and his ways past finding out!'
(Romans 11.33)

IT IS A GREAT LOSS to read the second commandment as
though it speaks only of the forbidding of pagan idol worship.
Obviously, it does prohibit idolatry, but really its chief purpose
it to forbid any attempt to make a representation of the true God. It
totally prohibits and condemns the worship of the true God
through any idol or picture of anything intended to depict Him. The
famous *Heidelberg Catechism* of 1563 asks, 'Must we, then, not make
any image at all?' Answer: 'God cannot and may not be imaged *[vis-
ibly portrayed]* in any way.' Then another question is asked: 'But
may not images *[depicting God or Christ]* be tolerated in churches as
books of the laity *[ie: teaching aids for the simple]*?' Answer: 'No, for

we should not be wiser than God, Who will not have His people taught by dumb idols, but by the lively preaching of His Word.'

We may surely use pictures of biblical events, particularly as visual aids for children, but never depicting the Father or the eternal Son (unless the latter is seen only indirectly, as explained later). But why may we not make any visual representation of God? Because in this second commandment God, by implication, is saying the following: 'Because I am the living, personal God, the infinite, eternal Spirit, you must never attempt to depict Me visually, for it is impossible to portray such attributes. The moment you reduce Me to a puny picture, or a lifeless image, you insult My attributes and set a small "god" in your mind.'

Illustrating God is Impossible

How can anyone illustrate the supreme Spirit Being? How can we portray One Who is infinite? What model or picture could convey even a hint of eternal existence, or unlimited wisdom and power? How could we represent God's sublime holiness and justice? Can we produce anything which is utterly flawless and stunningly perfect? And how could we even begin to depict unfathomable mercy and love? It is clear that any image or picture of God must fail to take Him seriously. However wonderful their gifts, human beings can only make images of God if their concept of God is vague, fleshly and inadequate.

Of course God is insulted by foolish and inadequate representations of Himself. No picture or sculpture stared at in worship can help us to focus our hearts upon God as the supreme Spirit, the God of infinite intelligence. The moment He is reduced to a visual representation, we are bound to lose all real awe and wonder at the almighty and glorious God. Only by the *words* which God has chosen to describe His attributes, may we gain a right impression of our great and glorious heavenly King, and so this second commandment is a crucial rule for the understanding of true worship.

Some Christians break this commandment unwittingly by having pictures of Christ, like the often-seen 'three-D' depiction of the Lord's Supper. This may be an expression of pious sentiment, but it is not really right. Believers would never use such pictures as a shrine, and worship before them, but they nevertheless possess a depiction of the eternal Son of God, which is wrong, because He is God. Pictures of Christ are usually Arian, even very Saxon, and whether drawn, painted or represented by an actor in a movie, the artist or actor must decide His build, features and expressions – about which we know nothing except that 'his visage was so marred more than any man,' and 'he hath no form nor comeliness; and when we shall see him, there is no beauty that we should desire him' *(Isaiah 52.14; 53.2)*. In any case His earthly life, the period of His humiliation, is over, and He now wears a glorified and glorious body, something of which may have been glimpsed in advance by three privileged disciples when He was transfigured before them *(Matthew 17.1-8)*. He may only be visualised very indistinctly in our minds, through a lens of deep respect, and never turned into a mere man of our imagination.

We should never lock Christ into His earthly manhood in the minds of the young, for in doing this we become no better than theological liberals who virtually limit Him to being a man. We would not object to a rear view of a robed figure with face concealed in, say, a Sunday School visual aid scene, but anything more shows no respect to the second commandment. If someone protests that there is no intention to worship through a picture of Christ, we reply that the commandment is not only to prevent false worship, but also to preserve a worthy concept of the divine Lord.

At this point it may be helpful to insert a plea to Bible Class leaders and Sunday School teachers. When the second commandment is explained there is a tendency to apply it by telling the children that idolatry is committed today when someone worships, say, a football idol or pop star instead of the Lord. While this is true, it should not be forgotten that the chief purpose of the commandment, namely, to draw attention to the divine attributes, is probably more interesting to the young. They are more impressed to hear that God forbids any representation of Himself because His 'nature' is too great to be drawn or depicted. People today do not know about the 'nature' of God, and that He is infinite, eternal, alive and personal, almighty, all-knowing and holy and just. They know nothing of His loving heart and His majesty, sovereignty and glory, and all this may be introduced through the second commandment.

Human Embellishments Banned in Worship

Another important lesson must be drawn from the prohibition of images, for by this commandment worship was made simple and spiritual, uncluttered by elaborate human ornamentation and gimmickry. We are effectively warned that we are allowed no scope to embellish the worship of God with unnecessary artistic trimmings and extras, because God has designed a way of worship by intelligent, heartfelt words, whether sung or said. In many passages the Bible indicates that we may have instrumental accompaniment, but today's artistic musical productions, exhibiting human skill and showmanship, and intended largely for pleasure, go way beyond accompaniment, tearing down the principle enshrined in the second commandment. Entertainment has taken over the worship of the Lord, and so much so that there is often no time even for Bible readings and prayer (of more than a couple of sentences). Many evangelicals wrongly believe that as long as they do not make stone scarabs they can never be guilty of breaking this commandment.

The second commandment is chiefly positive in drawing our

minds to the unillustratable attributes of God, and teaching us simplicity and spirituality of worship. This simplicity was confirmed very soon after the giving of the Commandments, when God gave instructions for the making of an altar (recorded in *Exodus 20.25*). He said, 'If thou wilt make me an altar of stone, thou shalt not build it of hewn stone: for if thou lift up thy tool upon it, thou hast polluted it.' Only God could make an atonement for sin, no 'work' or skill or artistry of the sinner being able to contribute or assist, and so the altar must be plain. The same applies to our worship. No ingenuity of ours must spoil it, whether imposing symbolic architecture, stained-glass windows, choirs singing complex and sophisticated musical arrangements, or modern entertainment spectaculars. All these things project human prowess (and pride) into worship, contrary to the second commandment. The prohibiting of visual representations of God also tells us that worship is by faith, and not by any attempted visualisation in our minds of, for example, the Saviour, or mere working up of sentimentality.

The worship of visual images requires not only skilful preparation of the image, but also mystical and imaginative skill. It demands considerable concentration to bring the image – or the god behind the image – to life. The monk in his cell stares at his crucifix, a lifeless image, but before his 'worship' can come to life he must engage in a sophisticated act of contemplation, imagination and emotion. With skill the monk will meditate, concentrating his thoughts on the crucifix, until, for him, it almost becomes the suffering Christ. He must 'worship' with this very special intensity to achieve fulfilment, and his act of meditation will (he may think) stand much to his credit, as a meritorious act.

By contrast, true worship by faith (rather than by attempted visualisation of Christ) is the simplest and humblest activity in which we can engage, yet the most glorious. Of course, worship requires effort, for we must prepare our hearts, humble ourselves, confess our sins, review our blessings, and rejoice before the Lord as He is revealed to us in His Word. Certainly, we must put earnestness and effort into worship, but if we possess spiritual life by conversion, our worship employs no phoney techniques to obtain satisfaction. Today we find musical groups and orchestras stirring up emotional feelings, but these are nothing other than 'audio-images', an alternative to heartfelt worship by words and by faith. The orchestra has become the image.

In the second commandment God takes away every possible form of image whether visual or audible, to remove all proud, skilful, man-centred, technique-driven worship. All man-made models and figures must go, and then the shutters of Heaven will roll aside so that we may perceive by faith the glory and greatness of our heavenly Father and of our Saviour. Then we shall see what Christ has done for us on Calvary's cross, and our humbled souls respond by admiring and loving Him from the heart. It is the simplest activity of the soul, but it can only take place if we are listening to God (speaking by His Word) and appreciating Him, not listening to, or looking at some product of our own ingenuity and artistry.

This commandment reflects the character of God, because all His communicating is direct and sincere, genuine and true. He does not use a civil service, or hide behind a screen of human imagery. When He commanded the people in Old Testament times to make a Tabernacle, then a Temple, representing His grace and the coming Christ, He chose the materials and symbols Himself, because accurate, untarnished self-revelation is part of His truthfulness.

The opposite positive virtue to the sin named in this commandment is faith, which is the basis of all acceptable communication with God. It is a choice between images or faith, because the former will always destroy the latter.

3

The Third Commandment
'Thou shalt not take the name of the Lord
thy God in vain.'

Keeping Close to the Lord

'This people draweth nigh unto me with their
mouth, and honoureth me with their lips;
but their heart is far from me.'
(Matthew 15.8)

THE REAL PURPOSE of the third commandment is gloriously positive, because it is designed to keep alive intelligent worship and truly close communion with the Lord. Sadly, many people seem to think that the sole meaning of this commandment is to condemn the use of God's name as a swear-word, and while it certainly does that, it goes much further, telling us *how* and in what spirit we should worship Him. Here God gives His redeemed people the policy they must follow lifelong in all their praying.

To appreciate the positive purpose of this commandment we must note the meanings of key words, considering first the word *take* – 'Thou shalt not *take* the name of the Lord thy God in vain.' The Hebrew literally means – *lift up*, referring to the lifting up of the voice to pronounce God's name in a religious manner, as in public prayer, the public reading of a scripture, or the singing of a hymn. The person who led the worship in Old Testament times 'lifted up' the name of the Lord. This commandment therefore refers to acts of public worship, although it obviously includes *any* pronouncing of the name of God in silent, personal prayer. The term – *in vain* – is translated from a Hebrew word which draws its meaning from the idea of a tempest rushing across the countryside leaving a desolate wasteland. The term means: *wasted, desolate, empty,* or vain and futile. Words that are said *in vain* have no positive thought in them. They are barren and void, because they are said without heartfelt sincerity, and are therefore trite or shallow words.

Do we sometimes say the name of the Lord like this, singing hymns, praying prayers or taking part in spiritual conversation using the name of God in a thoughtless or mechanical way? If the heart is low in sincerity, so that we have no real feeling for what we are saying, then in the sight of God the whole exercise becomes an empty charade, and not acceptable to Him. When we fall into cold and indifferent worship, do we realise that we are breaking the third commandment, or do we imagine that the commandment only deals with the blasphemous oaths of the unbeliever? The standard of this commandment applies to all our singing, praying and preaching, telling us that our minds and hearts must be completely behind what we are saying, otherwise we greatly offend the Lord.

We must especially notice that this commandment demands sincerity in connection with the Lord's *name.* God is evidently deeply concerned about the manner in which we name His name, but why? We do not mind too much if people use our names flippantly, so why should God be so concerned? The answer is that God's name is infinitely more important than any human name because it is His only description. Almighty God has no visible face or form, and we cannot see, touch, or feel Him in a physical manner, nor can we feel or perceive His divine essence. People may forget each other's names but they can see each other and shake hands, and even when a name does not immediately spring to mind, the existence of the other person is obvious. It is clear that the person is a man or a woman, tall or short, and possessing a distinctive appearance, so the *identity* of that person is not entirely dependent upon a name. But the name of God is much more important than any human name because it is by His name alone that we know Him and communicate with Him; it is His only identity, and the sole channel through which we focus our minds and hearts upon Him.

The Meaning of God's Name

A name is a *personal* appellation, and so by adopting a name the Lord assures us that He is a personal God Who may be communicated with. If God had no name we would have to become mystics engaging in the vague worship of an unknowable, hidden, amorphous 'force'. We would have to shut our eyes, empty our minds of all concepts, and worship in empty silence with shadowy ideas. Alternatively we would have to go to an art gallery and just stare at things that are beautiful, or gaze at the flowers and trees, and hope that somehow this would be acceptable as worship to the unknowable, impersonal 'force'. But by describing Himself through a name, God tells us that He is knowable and personal, because a name breathes communion and identity. Through His name we may approach Him in worship, love and prayer. We dare not use such a significant name lightly! We dare not pray or praise Him or sing to Him in such a way that His name registers no meaning to our souls.

God has chosen for Himself a name which is full of meaning, telling worshippers what they should have in their minds as they approach Him. That name is 'Lord', the Hebrew 'Jehovah', which means the 'self-existent and ever-existing One'. This name was announced by God in *Exodus 3.14* – 'I AM THAT I AM' – coming from the verb *to be* or *to exist*. God is self-existent in the sense that He does not have to obtain life and power from anyone or anything outside Himself. Further, He is the *only* self-existent Being, the source and fountain-head of *all* other life; the Creator of all that exists. He always has existed, and always will, and He is the supreme, unchanging God. THE LORD (Jehovah) means all this, and these are the thoughts we should have in our minds when we address Him. Not only do we have a *personal* God with a name, but His name tells us of His supreme and eternal power, and this should stir feelings of admiration and humble awe.

Another meaning of God's name flows out of this. If He is the source and sustainer of all existence, then He is the One to Whom we must turn for every blessing, for without Him we are lost. The second meaning of His name is therefore – *Father and Provider*. The very mention of God's name should remind us of His benevolent love and kindness. If we are tempted to conceit and self-sufficiency, His name will reprove and humble us, telling us that He is the sole fountain of life and power, without Whom we can accomplish nothing. Let us then name His name with insight and affection, always remembering that it means He is the great giver, and the answerer of prayer, Who helps and keeps His people in all circumstances.

Thirdly, the name of God speaks of His *authority*, for the supreme, self-existent Creator and Provider is beyond any shadow of doubt the Lord and Governor of the universe. As Creator He is obviously also the King, and we are creatures and servants. To lift up His name sincerely involves our recognising and submitting to Him as Lord of our lives, and anything less than wholehearted surrender will amount to lifting up His name in vain. To summarise, true worship involves 'lifting up' the name of the Lord with a sincere and respectful understanding of what it means. (1) We must consciously acknowledge His supreme, eternal life and power as the self-existent God. (2) We must acknowledge that He alone is the source and giver of everything we need, coming before Him as humble and needy people. (3) We must acknowledge Him as absolute Lord of our lives to Whom we owe our unreserved and unhesitating obedience and service.

We surely do not want to resemble the scribes and the Pharisees, whose worship was judged to be 'vain' (futile) by the Lord when He applied the words of Isaiah to them: 'Ye hypocrites, well did Esaias prophesy of you, saying, This people draweth nigh unto me with their mouth, and honoureth me with their lips; but their heart is far from me' *(Matthew 15.7-8)*. Yet whenever we name the name of God without the *meaning* of that glorious name registering in our hearts and minds, we play the hypocrite. Whenever we name the Lord God we *must* address Him as our personal Lord, realise afresh our total dependence upon Him, and dedicate ourselves to Him in absolute obedience.

When Sincere Worship Declines

1. A preoccupation with problems

What about those unworthy times when something spoils the feelingful and meaningful worship of the believer, especially the appreciation of the wonders of God's name? Perhaps some worrying problem absorbs all our emotional energy, so that as we sing hymns and pray, our thoughts are elsewhere and our words mechanical. Is it hypocrisy to be overwrought or preoccupied by cares? Not necessarily, but it certainly leads to hypocrisy if we allow ourselves to make a habit of it, or if we make no effort to combat it. When we come before our God we must respect Him, adore Him, and remember that He is watching us, for if we do not, we place ourselves on the high road to full-scale hypocrisy. What are these worries which sometimes steal from our worship? Are they so great that the God of all grace cannot help us? Do we praise Him with our lips and yet doubt His power to help? Why can we not lay our burdens at His feet and then worship Him with our hearts as well as our words?

2. A worldly spirit

Meaningless worship is also the inevitable result of a *worldly spirit*, and Satan will ensure that we are all tempted in this direction from time to time. It is possible for genuine believers to fall so far from simple living and self-denial that the prophet's words become true for them – 'With their mouth they shew much love, but their heart goeth after their covetousness' *(Ezekiel 33.31)*. God's name is named, but outside the house of God, or place of private prayer, the mind and the heart are taken up by personal dreams and desires. Perhaps someone just cannot wait to get out of the service to enjoy some new possession, or decorating plans and colour schemes engage the mind rather than thinking of the Lord. The sin of taking God's name in vain is certainly not limited to the unconverted person who blasphemes and swears. This commandment is much more seriously infringed when enlightened people pretend to worship when really their minds are on other things.

3. Disobedience to God

Hypocrisy in worship is frequently the result of a refusal to obey the Lord in some duty or calling. The offending Christian still comes to worship and engages in personal prayer, but is unwilling to keep certain vows or to yield entirely to Christ, because career has taken over the heart, or leisure and ease, or some specific sin. When witness opportunities arise, or Sunday School teachers are needed, or neighbourhood visitors, or the church needs repairs, cleaning or redecorating, such a Christian is seldom available. When he bows his head in prayer and addresses God by His familiar name – *Lord* – he does not mean what he says, because the Lord is no longer his supreme director, and he neither obeys nor serves Him. Having emptied the Lord's name of its meaning, he lifts it up thoughtlessly, and God will have to chastise him if he does not see his inconsistent behaviour and repent.

4. A lazy, casual approach

Another form of hypocrisy is seen when we sing hymns or pray in a *lazy* manner. Does our worship sometimes become merely a pleasant, light-hearted pastime which involves no great love, thought or effort? We sing up only if the tune pleases us, and we follow the service with only spasmodic flurries of attention as something unusual catches our interest. When the name of God is mentioned, our mind is not engaged in real gratitude and adoration, nor are we humbled and filled with awe. We do not feel our dependence upon Him, nor ask for any real spiritual blessings.

In many a church people may be seen peering around, taking stock of the building, whispering to each other, and making no apparent effort at all to focus mind and heart on the act of worship. All worship which is nominal or lazy is *vain*, and vain worship is a breach of the third commandment. A casual approach to the Lord is a disaster, yet today many ministers encourage it through their jokey leading of worship, their use of flippant, shallow language, and even their foolish use of over-casual dress. Informality is increasingly advocated in the world, but it will never co-exist with the awe and reverence which is stirred by an understanding of the meaning of the name of God.

5. False teaching is present

To consider another aspect of this, in denouncing the scribes and Pharisees, the Lord taught that worship is rendered vain when it is accompanied by false teaching, saying, 'In vain do they worship me, teaching for doctrines the commandments of men.' To say the name *Lord* with real meaning and sincerity, includes unreserved respect for His Word. The minister who spurns the Bible and its fundamental doctrines cannot possibly be serious when he uses the Lord's name, because he has no respect for God's authority. He is a law unto himself, picking and choosing what portions of God's Word he will accept and mingling them with the ideas of men.

Similarly, the Bible-believing evangelist or minister who lacks any sense of obligation to operate strictly by the Word in his methods of church growth, also empties the name of God of its meaning, for the Lord is no longer the sole source of power, and His Word no longer the exclusive blueprint for his methods. By adopting the gimmicks and ideas of men, and doing whatever he thinks fit, he cannot sincerely say *Lord*, for he is not listening to Him or obeying Him. If he feels that rock bands will make his work successful he goes ahead without consulting the supreme Governor of the Church, Whose name is *the Lord*. He then adds insult to injury by praying to the Lord, but he is not interested in working under His authority, and the word *Lord* is emptied of its meaning. Such a preacher may never use God's name as a swear-word, but in wresting from God His right to govern His church according to His wishes he has mentioned God's name lightly, and so breached God's law. All this is a mockery of the third commandment, which was designed to hold us safely and loyally under the Lord's authority. These words of Christ apply to evangelical workers today as much as to the Jews of the first century – 'And why call ye me, Lord, Lord, and do not the things which I say?' *(Luke 6.46).*

6. A discontented, grumbling spirit

One last example of vain worship must be mentioned because at some time it afflicts all believers. In *1 Corinthians 10.10*, the apostle Paul warns, 'Neither murmur ye', referring to the rejection of a generation of Israelites through this very sin. Grumbling and groaning is certain to turn our worship into a vain, desolate wasteland. If the word *Lord* includes the sense 'fountain of all good', how can we name that name while dominated by miserable, gloomy, self-pitying thoughts? While in this condition it is obvious that we do not believe the wonderful implications of the word, *Lord*, and therefore it fails to comfort and encourage us. We evidently do not really think that God is the supreme, ever-living God, Who is the source and supplier of all good, and the One Who has promised to hear our cries and be our eternal Friend. Murmuring, therefore, must be taken in hand before it makes us doubt God's wisdom and kindness, and name His name in an utterly thoughtless and empty way.

To summarise, the third commandment says: Never lift up God's glorious, wonderful name without thinking about its meaning and sincerely believing it. We realise it is not possible to do the fullest justice to God's name *every* time we utter it, but we can at least try. As long as our minds and hearts sincerely mean any one of the meanings of the Lord's name, we shall be able to utter it acceptably.

It may be that on one occasion our hearts feel very deeply that God is the exclusive source of life and power, the self-existent, eternal Being, while another time we may be touched by a special awareness that He is the God of all grace, source of all good, the One Who has given us in Christ salvation, life and strength, and on Whom we may depend for everything. Yet another time, we may be very conscious of the lordship aspect of His name, realising afresh that such a God is to be obeyed and served. If we do not feel or appreciate at least something of the meaning of God's name when we mention it, then we lift it up thoughtlessly and impudently, and break the third commandment.

While the standard may seem high, it is very kind, for if we truly understand what God's name means, and utter it with sincerity and yieldedness, we shall receive immeasurable blessing. God will draw us close to Himself and our worship will be filled with light, understanding, and an assurance that this God is our God. This precious commandment is provided to keep us close to Him.

How does this commandment reflect God's character? It does so because God's character is written into His name, as we have been observing through this chapter.

What are the other sins in the family of which vain, hypocritical mention of God's name is chief? All insincerity (in connection with God), together with thoughtlessness, shallowness, casual superficiality, mere formal worship, and hypocrisy. What are the opposite positive virtues to be sought after? Clearly – sincerity, thoughtfulness, reflection on God's attributes and grateful rejoicing.

4

The Fourth Commandment
'Remember the sabbath day, to keep it holy.'

The Believer's Special Day

'And upon the first day of the week,
when the disciples came together to break bread . . .'
(Acts 20.7)

THE FOURTH commandment, so pastoral and protective,
uniquely combines instruction, practical arrangements for
blessing and even prophecy in its scope. It is certainly a great
pity that some Bible teachers take the view that this commandment
largely lost its authority and purpose at the end of the Jewish era,
with the coming of Christ. Obviously there are major differences in
how this commandment is to be kept since the abolition of the types
and ceremonies of the Jewish law, but like all the other commandments, it is eternal moral law, reflecting the holy character and
requirements of God (as shown in our chapter end-note).

This commandment must one day bar the way to Heaven to all
people who denied their Creator any portion of their time and

respect. Irrespective of whether they ever had this commandment taught and explained to them, they will be judged by the *spirit* of its requirement, as it exposes the unreasonableness and hardness of their hearts. The fourth commandment will reveal that although people knew there must be a Creator from the very existence of the world, yet 'they glorified him not as God, neither were thankful; but became vain in their imaginations, and their foolish heart was darkened' *(Romans 1.21).*

Nothing could be more reasonable than that God should receive from rational, intelligent beings, all of whom are instinctually aware of His existence, some small corner of their time, and that they should enquire after Him and feel indebted to Him. In many nations, for much of the last two millennia, the Lord's Day has cast its influence over multitudes, who have known that here was an opportunity for seeking after their Creator. As God looks down from Heaven He sees the blatant appropriation of *every* hour and *every* day for self-worship, pleasure-worship and possession-worship, observing man's grim determination to yield nothing, not even a seventh of his life or thought, to his Maker. So the fourth commandment is appointed to stand alongside others as a flaming sword to keep and to guard the way that leads to the eternal realm. A sense of obligation to God was buried in man's conscience at creation, and this commandment will represent that obligation at the day of judgement.

The Nature of the Sabbath

While the fourth commandment plays its part in exposing the unreasonableness of sinful mankind, and guarding the gateway to eternal life, it was also designed to bring blessing and protection to God's redeemed people in every day and age. To appreciate this commandment's many benefits we must know the significance behind each word. '*Remember* the sabbath day,' simply means – 'Mark it; make it a day to be remembered in the years ahead.' Certainly the word *remember* points backwards to a number of matters (to be mentioned in due course), but it chiefly points forwards. Though the precise day of the week would change (the apostles were inspired to change it to 'the Lord's Day'), and though the strict ceremonial duties would be abolished in Christ, yet the setting aside of a day for worship and spiritual refreshment was to be observed by the Lord's people in future generations, wherever civil liberty would allow. The language of God is – *Remember!* . . . *never forget!* It is a duty for all men, but it is supremely a duty for the enlightened people of God. This day, as we shall see, is God's right, crucial for the health of our own souls, and a vital part of our witness.

The meaning of the term *sabbath day* throws light on the purpose behind the command, although there is disagreement about the *total* meaning of the word, which is why we have the untranslated Hebrew word *shabbat* employed in our English translations. The essential meaning is to rest, to leave off doing something, to bring something to an end, or even to commemorate or celebrate something. However, it also refers to a period of change, like an intermission or interval. Taking these terms together, the Sabbath day is an intermission in which we stop or cease our usual activities to do something else. It does not necessarily mean 'rest' in the purely physical sense, as though the Sabbath was a time for putting one's feet up and going to sleep. We know this, for in *Exodus 20.11* the Lord bases the Sabbath command on His own example, telling us that after the six days of creation activity He 'rested the seventh day'. The parallel passage in *Exodus 31.17* actually uses the *sabbath* verb: 'For in six days the Lord made heaven and earth, and on the seventh day he rested [*Hebrew: shabbat*], and was refreshed.' This helps us to understand what is meant by *rest*, for Almighty God never slumbers nor sleeps, nor grows weary or exhausted.

The Lord's people sometimes find Sunday rather busy as they worship, receive and give instruction from the Word, gather and teach Sunday School children, and entertain guests for the evangelistic service, not to mention the ferrying of elderly and distant people as well as children to services. In these circumstances they may ask plaintively, 'Is this not supposed to be a day of rest?' The answer is that it is a day of rest from our *normal labour*. It is an intermission or interlude for the most refreshing activity in the world, a day in the courts and in the service of the King of Heaven, and just as a good holiday may be extremely active, so should the Lord's Day include spiritual activity for His glory.

More significantly, the reference made to God 'resting' after His creative activity reminds us of our need of spiritual refreshment. Although the Lord needs no refreshment, He assumes a human stance to teach us that we need to draw aside from this world, and be refreshed by heavenly things. Just as God stopped creating, we lay aside our ordinary affairs, lift our eyes above the hustle and bustle of created things, and focus upon the Creator. It is a time of reflection and worship and service when everything is for the Lord, and so long as society allows us to have such a day, this is what we must do. So let us stop, set aside all secular affairs, and engage in wonder, reflection, praise and service.

Activities for the Lord's Day

The next word in the fourth commandment is very challenging – 'Remember the sabbath day, to *keep it . . .*' The Hebrew word used here is not quite the same as our word *keep*, for it means more than *retain* or *maintain* or *honour* some appointment. The Hebrew word *keep* means 'hedge about' perhaps with a protective hedge of thorns, to guard and protect something. God says we must not allow any erosion of the Sabbath, and by implication we are warned that Satan will attempt to ruin our use of this special day, and we must watch for and resist his temptations. This very week many believers throughout the world will be tempted to get entangled with secular or unnecessary activities on the Lord's Day. Obviously we must be very understanding in the case of believers who are compelled to work on the Lord's Day, there being no other way open to them of earning a living and feeding their families. But to whatever extent we are able to set aside some or all of this day, we must in conscience keep it for Him.

The next word to consider is – *holy*, which means clean, consecrated, special, and given to God. On all other days spiritual things have to be shared with secular affairs, and the latter take the lion's share of our time and energy, but this day should not be shared with earthly pursuits. This obviously includes many cultural and leisure activities which a Christian may legitimately follow six days of the week, but the Lord's Day is to be as special as it can be, and many otherwise wholesome recreational activities should have no place in it. On a church young people's holiday, for example – aside from worship – fellowship activities such as walking and talking should be substituted for football and board games. On this day also, in every believing home, the television is best left firmly off. On the Lord's Day we do not attend a service of worship and then listen to a symphony. Earthly distractions, even good ones, which are solely for pleasure, should not get through the hedge or fence we place around the Lord's Day.

These days it is common for Christian people to snort at the idea of sacred song, and many want to make the music of worship as similar as possible to the music of the present-day morally debased entertainment industry. They laugh at the concept of worship as something completely different, and separate from the world, regarding the musical forms of traditional evangelical worship as outdated. But the Sabbath commandment gives its weight to the many other Scripture passages which mark worship out as *different, holy, special,* and *set apart.* Our worship on the Lord's Day is different, even culturally distinctive, all this being taught in the Sabbath commandment. Worship supremely belongs to the Lord's Day when all the usual pursuits stop, and we do things differently, and God's day must never be conformed to the world. We do not seek our own enjoyment at an earthly level, even in legitimate ways, because we are to keep the day *holy* or special, or set apart for the Lord's affairs – worship, instruction, service, and fellowship. The believing student will make every endeavour not to study on this day; the television, as we have urged, will be left alone, and the hours of the day will be a special time for the things of the Lord.

Obviously a dedicated day needs preparation, as in ancient times. We remember that the Jews of old were an agricultural people, and therefore all their work programmes had to be arranged with this day in mind. The same applies today with the planning of domestic duties, such as shopping, cleaning and major cooking, and also with student assignments due for submission on Monday, all being completed by the end of Saturday.

Even Sunday fatigue needs to be considered, because some people are seriously affected by the change of lifestyle between Saturday and Sunday. As soon as they sit down in God's house they fall asleep. They ought to prepare somehow for the change by whatever helps them, such as earlier cessation of activity on the previous day. Some believers court disaster by allowing the chores of Saturday to drag into the early hours of Sunday, so that they bring exhausted and uninterested hearts to the Lord on the greatest day of the week. If the day is not prepared for, and there is no mental liveliness, then it cannot be truly remembered, observed, guarded, kept, sanctified or hallowed for the Lord, but instead becomes, as it were, the 'rubbish bin' day of the week when we are least alert, fervent and responsive.

The fourth commandment tells us that 'the Lord blessed the sabbath day', and we naturally enquire – in what sense did the Lord *bless* it? He made it a day of spiritual benefit, clothing it with blessings that no other day has. If some tremendous political upheaval took place in the land, and for some reason Thursday was declared to be the national day off instead of Sunday, this would not greatly upset true Christians for we are not legalistic about these matters. With Calvin we would say that it does not matter to us which day we observe as the Lord's Day, for we know that, if liberty allows, any day given to God will be blessed by Him in a wonderful way, and we shall know the unction and power of *Isaiah 58.13-14*:

> 'If thou turn away thy foot from the sabbath, from doing thy pleasure on my holy day; and call the sabbath a delight, the holy of the Lord, honourable; and shalt honour him, not doing thine own ways, nor finding thine own pleasure, nor speaking thine own words: then shalt thou delight thyself in the Lord; and I will cause thee to ride upon the high places of the earth, and feed thee with the heritage of Jacob thy father.'

Six Purposes of the Lord's Day

Here are six purposes for which the Lord's Day has been established for as long as time endures, all of which are derived both from the commandment of Sinai and the example of the Lord's Day observance in the New Testament.

1 Firstly, this commandment provides a regular season for gratitude and worship, when God's people pay their spiritual vows to their God and King, directing to Him their appreciation and adoration.

2 Secondly, this commandment calls believers to consider and study the Lord, reflecting upon, inquiring into and learning more about the faith once delivered. They are to be challenged by His Word, moved in heart, drawn closer to Him, amazed and

thrilled by the Word, and built up in understanding and doctrine. It is above all others the day for spiritual growth.

3 Thirdly, through the Lord's Day Christians *establish their priori-ties* and give a demonstration of their obedience. Just as the Jews of old had to organise their lives around this day so that their agricultural and business programmes bowed and yielded to the things of God, so we 'disrupt' our normal activities and do likewise. In this we pledge our programmes to God, and declare that His will counts most in our lives. Our lives, and 'secular' pleasures are subordinated to the Lord on this precious day.

4 Fourthly, the Lord's Day is a dramatic and significant day of testimony. When the Jews of old organised their lives around this day, a great impact was made upon their growing youngsters and also upon the nations round about. All would ask, 'Who is this supreme Lord for Whom this day is yielded?' Similarly today, where the Lord's people are seen worshipping God, preaching the Gospel and leaving alone garden, car-washing, shopping and self-pleasing on the Lord's Day, a great witness is established before the watching world. This also is the day for evangelistic Sunday Schools and evangelistic adult services, so that, ideally, for 52 Sundays every year, there is one service to which we invite unconverted people. It is above all others the day of the Gospel. The converted student living in a hall of residence, who yields to temptation and spends most of Sunday as if it were a weekday, little realises what witness he forfeits. Unsaved people may not show it, but they are certainly affected by the attachment of believers to the Lord's Day. For families also, this commitment to the Lord often helps prove the sincerity of believers to neighbours, relations and doubting children.

5 Fifthly, the Lord's Day is especially significant as a declaration of total dependence upon God for grace and help. The Old

Testament Jew may well have pleaded that he needed more time to harvest his crop or sow his seed. What a commercial setback the Sabbath represented, but in keeping it the people told the Lord that His blessing was more significant to them than self-reliance. Similarly, today, there are so many things Christian people could be engaged in to ensure the success of their affairs. They could (they may think) solve so many problems and accomplish so much more if only they could plunder time from this day. But the Lord's Day is our statement to God that we depend upon His mercy, power and help. This day is an act of commitment which signals our trust to Heaven in more eloquent language than words.

6 Sixthly, we make another declaration to God through keeping the Lord's Day, namely, our great desire for the eternal Sabbath, for the Sabbath is given partly as a foretaste and figure of heavenly glory. On the Lord's Day we demonstrate to God that we really want the return of Christ and the ushering in of the eternal order. We grasp eagerly at the foretastes of Heaven that we are invited to enjoy week by week. To disdain the Lord's Day is to show that we are not among those who look for and 'love his appearing'. The nominal evangelical who worships once on Sunday and then goes back to the television is only revealing a preference for this world over the next. The 'Sabbath rest' is a token, foretaste or sign of what God has promised, as the hymnwriter expressed in these lines –

> *We bless Thee for this earnest*
> *Of better rest above,*
> *This token of Thy kindness,*
> *This pledge of boundless love.*
>
> *O Lord, again we bless Thee*
> *For such a day as this,*
> *So rich in ancient glories,*
> *So bright with hope of bliss.*
>
> *Thomas Vincent Tymms*

The Lord's Day is a kind test of our attitude on all these points. If the unbeliever will be judged by the spirit of the commandment, where will the believer stand? We hear nowadays of evangelical churches having only one service on the Lord's Day, even claiming that there is no scriptural warrant for more, and insisting that the remainder of the day is for relaxation and personal pleasure. How we should value and appreciate the blessings which the Lord has designed for us in a day given to guard our souls, supply our needs, and lift us to Heaven. No wonder this is one of the two commandments out of ten which is expressed in a wholly positive way – 'Remember the sabbath day, to keep it holy.' It is its own 'opposite positive virtue'.

The Lord's Day clearly reflects the character and heart of God because it is a token of what He wills and plans for His people eternally, a realm of worship, communion, and spiritual light.

Neglect of the Lord's Day in a sense heads a family of offences – sins such as lack of commitment, unspiritual priorities, omission of devotions, and disobedience of practical duties for Christian living. The Lord's Day leads the way in establishing the believer's attitude to all these matters.

The Status of the Fourth Commandment

Some have claimed that the fourth commandment is the 'odd man out' in the decalogue. They feel that it belongs with the ceremonial regulations which were binding only upon the Jews during the period of the Old Testament, while their 'national covenant' was in force. This point of view is in collision with three invincible arguments:–

(1) The unique status of the Ten Commandments as an expression of the *everlasting* principles of righteousness, written with the finger of God.

(2) The statement that the Sabbath is a 'creation ordinance' in *Exodus 20.11*. God hallowed the principle of such a day from the beginning.

(3) The inauguration of the *Lord's Day* as the New Testament expression of the commandment, as seen in the practice of the early church (eg: *Acts 20.7; 1 Corinthians 16.2; Revelation 1.10*).

5

The Fifth Commandment
'Honour thy father and thy mother.'

God's Plan for His Church

'That it may be well with thee,
and thou mayest live long on the earth.'
(Ephesians 6.3)

THE FIFTH commandment suffers greatly from being taken only at its literal face value. What God meant in a very comprehensive way, we so often interpret in a very narrow, limited way, and so escape the full responsibility which God has laid upon us. In this chapter we will be emphasising the application which this commandment has to life in the churches of Christ, rather than the primary sense of the words which are fairly well understood.

Perhaps we do not regard this commandment as one of the most important, because murder is infinitely more serious than the failure to honour father and mother, and adultery is also a much graver crime. With this in mind we may hold the fifth commandment in fairly low esteem, and so we need to be jolted by the surprising remark of the apostle Paul –

> 'Honour thy father and mother; (which is the first commandment with promise;) that it may be well with thee, and thou mayest live long on the earth' *(Ephesians 6.1-3).*

At first glance Paul seems to be wrong, because the second commandment was the first to have a promise attached to it. But Paul undoubtedly means that it was first in the sense of being the *chief* commandment for the securing of long life and well-being. In other words, we may paraphrase the commandment as quoted by Paul to read: 'Honour thy father and mother, which is the most important commandment *as far as its promise is concerned* – that it may be well with thee, and that thou mayest live long on the earth.'

If someone is very ill, the most important thing is to get that person to a doctor, and if someone wants to learn, the most important place to be is the school or college. If we are seeking the longevity and stability of families, or society at large, then the most important factor is the fifth commandment. If this surprises us it is because we have greatly underestimated the meaning and value of this part of God's holy and marvellous law.

Stability or Longevity?

Let us think, for a moment, about the promise which is attached to the commandment in *Exodus* – 'that thy days may be long upon the land which the Lord thy God giveth thee'. In *Deuteronomy 5.16* this promise is expanded to include the words quoted by Paul in *Ephesians 6* – 'that it may be well with thee'. Is it really so, that if we honour our parents things will go well with us and we will live long lives? Not necessarily, because the fulfilment spoken of in *Exodus* and *Deuteronomy* was not the individual's life-span, but the length of years for which the Israelites would occupy the land of promise,

including their well-being as a nation. The words of the commandment are – 'that thy days may be long upon the land which the Lord
thy God giveth thee'. The promise says that the Israelites would
enjoy a long and stable occupation of that great tract of land if they
observed God's commandment to give honour and reverence to the
parental generation, giving due respect to their teaching, leadership
and experience. While the commandment is addressed to individuals, the promise undoubtedly refers chiefly to the stability and
longevity of the family or social unit. Obedience to this commandment meant that God would bless, and they would have a
well-ordered and secure society which would not degenerate into
chaos, indiscipline and dissipation.

The way the apostle Paul applies the commandment to children
shows that there is also a personal aspect to the promise, and we
should certainly not interpret this away. God will honour and bless
in a special way – subject to His will for individuals – those who
maintain respect and care for their parents, whenever this is possible. If we desire spiritual blessing and usefulness throughout our
allotted days, and our parents are not antagonistic or over-demand-
ing and domineering, we had better be sure that we are obeying and
pleasing the Lord at this point. God counts it a great sin when offspring are headstrong, ungrateful and callous, discarding the
elderly, and denying them respect, concern and support.

Chiefly, however, the promise of long life relates, as we have seen,
to the stability and survival of the nation of Israel in their new land,
and because Israel typifies and depicts the church, it relates also to
the blessedness and stability of church life. God, in effect, says to the
Israelites, and by extension to believers in New Testament churches:
'If within your nation [church] you have great respect for the parental generation, for your leaders, for your right traditions, for
instruction, guidance and counsel, then as a nation [church] you will
be stable, successful, and will long occupy the land and endure to

serve Me.' The application to churches today is obvious. If we understand and honour God's principles for government, order, guidance and leadership, then our churches will be stable and blessed. They will long occupy the 'land' of Truth which the Lord gives them, not losing their lampstand, or ceasing to proclaim the everlasting Gospel.

'Parents' in the Broadest Sense

But how do we get from 'father and mother' to church government? By observing how the Old Testament uses the word *father* and *mother*, it is easily demonstrated that the fifth commandment is meant to be applied in a broader way to all types of parent, including spiritual guides. In *Genesis 45*, Joseph tells his brothers that God made him a 'father to Pharaoh'. Obviously he was not Pharaoh's father in a literal sense, but this early passage in the Bible helps us to understand the very broad sense in which the word *father* was often used. In this case it meant that Joseph became Pharaoh's counsellor and prime minister.

In the book of *Judges* we find the word *mother* used in a similar way, for we are told that Deborah became a 'mother in Israel'. Because she was a judge and prophetess, a guide and leader, she was called a *mother*. We remember how Elisha cried out to Elijah, 'My father, my father!' It was normal and customary for him to address his teacher by this term, although Elijah was not his literal father, but his leader and mentor, and also the principal of the school of the prophets. King Joash does exactly the same to Elisha, proving that it was common practice. 'My father, my father,' he cries out to Elisha, because he was a prophet, pastor and counsellor.

In Old Testament times the parental terms were used flexibly for various offices, both spiritual and civil, and in the New Testament Paul uses the word *father* in the same way, saying to the Corinthians,

'I have begotten you by the Gospel . . . you have many teachers but you do not have many fathers.' Thomas Watson represents the Puritan tradition in his exposition of the Ten Commandments when he divides this commandment into five sections, distinguishing between *political* fathers, *ancient* fathers, *spiritual* fathers, *domestic* fathers (by which he means masters of servants, or employers), and last of all, *natural* fathers. How superficial we are today by comparison, when we read this commandment and see only *natural* fathers. So we learn that the commandment is very broad, and most certainly includes application to leadership in the churches.

The Meaning of 'Honour'

What kind of respect is meant by the word 'honour' as used in this commandment? Certainly, it does not refer to servile obedience to people simply because they hold office, or happen to be older than we are. What, for example, should the attitude of the Christian be to political rulers? The answer of the Bible is that we are subject to them, except when it means disobeying God. We pay taxes and we pray for them, that there may be peace and freedom from persecution. We are subject to them irrespective of party, but we have no obligation to admire them at a personal level, or to agree with their political theory. Indeed, how could we, because many, if not most of them, are as far away from biblical thinking as Nero was when Paul wrote his instructions about our attitude to civil leaders (in *Romans 13.1-7* and *1 Timothy 2.1-4*). The Christian is not a social revolutionary or a rebel. He is meek and subordinate, obedient and respectful, yet if the civil ruler commands something which is against God's law, then the believer will follow God's Word even unto death. Nevertheless, he maintains his respect and obedience to lawful authority, and prays for leaders because he knows that national leadership is intended by God for stability and justice. We cannot here enter into the issue of whether social revolution is ever justifiable, although certain great divines have argued for its validity in extreme circumstances.

There are also some exceptions attached to our honouring of natural parents, for we remember that the Saviour said to the man who wished to delay his discipleship in order to bury his father, 'Let the dead bury their dead,' and to the multitudes, 'If any man come to me, and hate not his father, and mother . . . he cannot be my disciple' *(Luke 9.60; 14.26)*.

Honouring parents (especially unreasonable, unbelieving parents) does not involve buckling in to their various schemes to loosen their offspring from their dedicated walk. If parents (sometimes even Christian parents) are possessive, overbearing, or domineering, their adult children are not obliged to invest undue time and energy pandering to them and trying to please them, fearing that to do otherwise would be a breach of God's commandment. Believers have a priority for zealous service in their local church. They have to honour the Lord first and foremost, and their responsibility to honour parents comes second to their duty to God. Devotion to parents, therefore, must in no way challenge devotion to God. We give respect and care, but not at heavy cost to the Lord.

Some young couples compromise themselves and their testimony to unbelieving parents by accepting valuable gifts, handouts and help from them, often with unwholesome results. The parents may think they score over the God of their children, for they proudly think that these only have well-being and settled circumstances by the grace of their parents. Abraham's words to the king of Sodom are significant here: 'I will not take any thing that is thine, lest thou shouldest say, I have made Abram rich' *(Genesis 14.23)*. Equally seriously, the offspring feel obliged to fit in with all the demands of such parents on account of what they have received. *Honour* does not mean – become dependent, indebted or obligated.

Authority in a Congregation

The organising of our churches is ultimately founded on the law of this fifth commandment, and we now look at some of the ways in which it protects our church life. Those who lead churches – spiritual parents – are to be credited with significance and experience in our estimation of them. The word 'honour' means that we invest people with importance and value. We are not to clothe leaders with *personal* authority, or infallibility, nor are we to give them authority over our individual affairs, but we are to extend respect, listen to them, and follow their scriptural lead. This is a vital protection against problems and evils arising either through anarchy or through the inexperience and instability of youth. Imagine what a church would be like if, from the moment of conversion, we were all able to do whatever seemed right in our own eyes, introducing every idea that flashed through the mind into the worship and witness of the church. The result these days would be (and sadly is, in many churches) worldliness and crazy gimmicks. So God has imposed a principle of leadership and guidance to stabilise the churches and to protect them from impulsiveness, rashness and inexperience, however well-intended the ideas proposed (see, for example, *Hebrews 13.7, 13.17* and *1 Timothy 3.6*). It is through soundness, good sense, and the resulting stability that the promise of the commandment is fulfilled – 'That your days may be long in the land'.

The fifth commandment also protects the young from pride and arrogance, by calling for respect for elders, and preventing them from doing as they want. We realise that elders and senior members in a church get things wrong, and they are not to be regarded as infallible, but we give the Lord's structure precedence unless there are clear biblical reasons why we should not. In God's plan for a Gospel church young people and young believers are not accelerated into dizzy heights of authority and ministry or other public activities before time, so that pride takes over, and a spiritual fall follows (as described by Paul in *1 Timothy 3.6*).

It is an obvious violation of the spirit of the fifth commandment for a church to push people into responsibility or service when they are barely out of the spiritual cradle. This is not merely an error of judgement, it is the flouting of a commandment which carries as much authority as those against murder and adultery, yet early elevation to leadership and ministry is common in churches today. Churches are buckling before the tidal wave of rock music, and in numerous places the pulpit frequently yields to a 'platform' of youngsters parading their skills and entertaining. This is a simultaneous transgression of more than one commandment, and it is certainly a direct attack on God's insistence on mature leadership, government and guidance in the worship, teaching and pastoral care activities of His churches.

The fifth commandment also establishes in the church a method for discipline, because it authorises 'parents' to discipline, guide and lead. We take note of the fact that the commandment says, 'Honour thy father and thy mother', mentioning both because the guidance of the church involves not only authority and discipline, but also love and care. The parental picture is very apt and precious here, for fathers and mothers have their growing children on their hearts. Their concern is for behaviour, but they also feel for their children. Should any be injured or go astray, parents feel the burden very deeply, and it is the same in the church. Spiritual leaders must possess affection, sympathy and understanding, and be jealous to protect and encourage the people of God. Within the household of God there is always a generation leaving youth behind and moving gradually into the maturer age-band, and these members should be drawing around them the mantle of care, concern, responsibility, affection and love, for they are now moving from the *honouring* of spiritual parents to the *exercising* of spiritual parenthood.

Leadership Rejected in the Last Days

In describing the social fragmentation of the 'last days' (in *2 Timothy 3*), Paul particularly mentions that people will be 'disobedient to parents'. In other words they will be unsubmissive to all levels of parent, whether leaders of society, natural parents, church elders or long-held biblical traditions which deserve careful respect. People will, alongside this, be 'unthankful', and this would include proud believers who seem entirely indifferent to the human source of all their blessings and benefits. Paul later mentions people who are 'heady' and 'highminded', by which he means reckless and blinded with conceit. Having no time for God's order, such people bring endless upheaval and instability into society, and often into Christ's churches also. These are undoubtedly the days in which we now live, and we must encourage one another not to allow the spirit of this present world to spill into the life of our churches. The fifth commandment is provided for the comfort and preservation of society, but chiefly for the church, and for the curbing of selfish, ambitious sins, and for the survival of a truly Christian lifestyle and culture. The spiritual longevity of a blessed church depends upon it.

This is the second of the positive commandments, so it is its own 'opposite positive virtue'. Its opposite negative vice is disdain of parental authority at any level – in family life, national life, or church life. The fifth commandment reflects God's character because the extending of respect and honour is part of His own being, as we see in the perfect unity and harmony of the members of the Triune Godhead. The eternal realm of glory will see how God will have drawn all redeemed people, and the holy angelic host, into a state of undying and unblemished obedience and adoration of Himself. This is His great plan, according to His holy character and will.

6

The Sixth Commandment
'Thou shalt not kill.'

Murderers All!

' . . . lest there be debates, envyings, wraths,
strifes, backbitings, whisperings, swellings, tumults.'
(2 Corinthians 12.20)

IF THERE IS a commandment which the majority of people have never transgressed it is the sixth – or so they may think. In countries at peace, murder is considered to be a minority crime, but as we have already repeatedly noted, each named sin in the Ten Commandments is only the chief of a family of offences. To see only literal murder in this commandment is to greatly limit the message which God intended, as Christ showed in the Sermon on the Mount, when He taught that *hatred* is a breach of this commandment. Our first task is to identify the 'murder' sins, and then to explore the *opposite positive virtues* of these sins, and to set our sights on these. Some comments on abortion as a form of murder will be made at the end of this chapter.

When the Saviour opened out the application of this commandment to include anger, hatred and contempt toward others, He was not telling His hearers anything new, or adding a meaning which Old Testament believers would never have imagined. He was simply drawing attention to what Moses had taught when the commandment was first given. (And who was Moses, but a man inspired by Christ, the real author?)

Moses Expands the Murder Sins

Soon after Moses had delivered the Ten Commandments to the people, he was given by God a number of additional regulations, including a list of offences punishable by death, the first of these being murder *(Exodus 21.12)*. This is immediately followed by four other crimes meriting the death sentence, all very definitely linked closely with murder, though at first sight they may seem to have little in common. Violent behaviour toward father or mother merited death (even though neither had died), and so did the crime of kidnap or slave-trading, and the act of cursing one's parents (which no doubt involved disowning them and withholding support in old age). If someone hurt a woman with child, and the child was lost, the assailant was to lose his life. It is clear from this grouping of crimes that Moses was dealing with offences which were in the same general sin-family as murder.

But how did the abuse and humiliation of parents, for example, come to be included in this murder family of sins? The obvious answer is that such conduct 'murdered' the self-respect, dignity and well-being of those parents. We remember that in the ancient eastern family, if adult children disowned and humiliated their parents, they took away from them all meaningful reason for existence. Those ageing parents were entitled to honour, family companionship and support, and their happiness and joy was vested in their family. To be stripped of all this was a form of murder, being an act of hatred which tore away from parents something as precious as life itself.

Similarly, to show such contempt for another person that one would deprive him of his liberty, and capture him for slavery, was a sin in the same family as murder. It is clear that Moses taught that the sixth commandment encompassed a group of crimes in which rejection, abasement and contempt struck out at the vital well-being and liberty of others. We should not therefore think that the Lord Jesus, in later times, tampered with the ancient law, or made adjustments to it, or added to it, for the things which the Saviour taught had always been there for the people to see. The Lord, after all, wrote the Old Testament in the first place, and He knew what it was intended to convey.

Moses Adds Hatred and Slander

Leviticus 19 also contains a detailed application of several of the Ten Commandments and throws further light on how the people were taught to think. In this chapter Moses freely interweaves commands prohibiting hatred, slander and gossip with those against murder and vengeance, showing yet again that these offences are all in the same general family. He says – 'Thou shalt not go up and down as a talebearer among thy people: neither shalt thou stand against the blood of thy neighbour *[ie: act against the life of thy neighbour]* . . . Thou shalt not hate thy brother in thine heart' *(Leviticus 19.16-17).*

The same coupling up of thoughts occurs in the very next verse, where the crime of murderous vengeance is placed in the same category as hostile resentment, feuding, or bearing grudges: 'Thou shalt not avenge, nor bear any grudge against the children of thy people, but thou shalt love thy neighbour as thyself' *(Leviticus 19.18).*

Apparently, in the law of Moses, the taking of life was the chief and worst offence of a whole family of 'hate' sins which included gossip, slander, malicious scheming, enslavement, moral 'destruction' of parents, grudges, and similar things. So when the Lord Jesus Christ expounds the law in *Matthew 5*, He says precisely what He had said before through the lips of Moses, showing the Jews what they should have understood all along:

> 'Ye have heard that it was said by them of old time, Thou shalt not kill; and whosoever shall kill shall be in danger of the judgment: but I say unto you, That whosoever is angry with his brother without a cause shall be in danger of the judgment: and whosoever shall say to his brother, Raca, shall be in danger of the council: but whosoever shall say, Thou fool, shall be in danger of hell fire. Therefore if thou bring thy gift to the altar, and there rememberest that thy brother hath ought against thee; leave there thy gift before the altar, and go thy way; first be reconciled to thy brother' *(Matthew 5.21-24).*

Here it is confirmed to us that the sixth commandment includes hatred in the heart, and anger without just cause. The insults mentioned by the Lord were not light-hearted abuse, or momentary outbursts of anger, but hate-ridden, deliberately wounding, cutting insults. To say, 'Raca!' was evidently an expression of contempt intended to humiliate, so that someone was totally crushed and set aside as worthless. In a sense, 'moral' murder was committed through contempt and disregard, and so the sixth commandment was broken. 'Thou fool!' was equally intended to inflict maximum hurt and rejection.

Emotional Murder Today

Have we broken the sixth commandment? 'Never!' we may reply, because we have never killed a person, but this is to hide behind the letter of the law, because all are guilty of contempt, disdain, hatred, anger, slander, scheming against others, gossip, grudges, and even sometimes the hurtful setting aside of parents. And what about enslavement? Is there anyone, perhaps a member of our household, who has been virtually deprived of liberty, happiness and fulfilment because of our overbearing, selfish and heartless manner of life?

In some periods of our history it has been the cultural norm for husbands to take away the liberty of their wives, rendering their lives menial and meaningless. Even today some Christian husbands tread down the gifts and spiritual service potential of their wives, treating them as inferior in every way. The sixth commandment places this in the murder family of sins, for such behaviour selfishly demoralises and denigrates another person. Obviously, it is not as serious as murder, but it is in the same class of sin. Slavery and serfdom in all their forms, including a grotesque attitude to marriage, are seen in this commandment as moral murder.

Murder includes in its family the denial of affection and self-respect to another; the destruction of reputation, and the extinguishing of liberty and happiness. In the light of this, how do we stand in relation to the sixth commandment? May it be, for many, a schoolmaster to bring us back to the throne of grace for pardon and renewed character.

Without conversion, most people (especially after mid-twenties) develop deep hatred for certain others, and spend much of their lives driven by hostility or envy. But even after conversion there is a remnant of these attitudes left within us, and this we must strive to subdue, by the help of God, so that wherever possible, we may be people of love, kindness, peace and reconciliation. The sixth commandment addresses this vital department of our sanctification.

The apostle Paul groups these related sins together just as Moses did, and the Saviour. In *2 Corinthians 12.20*, for instance, we read this remarkable list of offences: 'debates *[quarrelling]*, envyings, wraths, strifes, backbitings, whisperings, swellings *[superiority that belittles others]*, tumults'. Is not the 'murder-hate' family easily recognisable in this sorry catalogue of argument, hostility, anger, temper, gossip, slander and factiousness, in which people morally put one another to death, and effectively kill the Lord's work at the same time? Do unloving and wrongly contentious people in a local church realise their guilt before God for smashing the sixth commandment? Do vindictive gossips realise that God has already framed a charge against them – a crime in the murder-hate family?

At the risk of labouring the point, we see Paul once again grouping together the murder-hate sins in his 'works of the flesh' list in *Galatians 5.20-21*, where he names – 'Hatred, variance, emulations, wrath, strife, seditions, heresies, envyings, murders'. To prove the point still further, consider Paul's sin list in *Romans 1.29-30*, where he groups together – 'Maliciousness . . . envy, murder, debate, deceit, malignity; whisperers, backbiters, haters of God, despiteful'. The gallery of sins is the same as in the two other lists.

It is an important and challenging exercise to reflect on why these sins must be regarded as the younger brothers and sisters of murder. We have not committed literal murder, but many of our deeds bear the family likeness. All the offences mentioned in the apostle's lists *murder* relationships between believers, and *kill* deep spiritual harmony in the church. They are all destructive acts, calculated to hurt, maim and destroy another person, or many people, in some way.

Take whisperings and backbitings, which are callous, hostile remarks or tales whispered in confidential tones against people behind their backs. The reputations of targeted people are murdered, and the Lord's prescribed way of dealing with offences is trampled to death at the same time. The loving spirit of those who hear vindictive gossip is also destroyed, for there are few more infectious evils than backbiting. Strife, or quarrelsomeness, is an obvious murderer of fellowship and service for the Lord. Quarrelsomeness soon leads to *wrath*, translated from a Greek word which literally means – *heavy breathing*. This is sheer animal temper, which gives rise to commotion, trampling, cutting, dividing, often without the slightest effort at self-control, and without any conscience about the spiritual carnage or hurt caused to the Lord's work. Where else could such a sin be listed other than under the banner of murder? When we next see a person who is a spoiler of the peace, harmony and witness of a fellowship, let us be clear that such a person is committing sins in the murder-hate category.

When we enter into church membership we pledge and bind ourselves to be united with our brothers and sisters in the Lord according to the rules of Christ. We make (or should make) solemn promises to God that we will process all our problems, complaints and offences in the way laid down in Scripture, and in the spirit of meekness and progress. But some believers disregard these standards (together with their promises and vows) the moment it suits them. Perhaps some offence has been suffered by them, or they develop a disagreement with others in the church, but because pride is involved they refuse to seek a solution in the biblical way and launch instead into backbiting or even open hostility. Obviously others will be hurt and relationships fractured, and the work of God impeded because the Spirit is grieved. It may be quite a 'low level' of vindictiveness, but it is still in the murder-hate class of offences.

Envyings, and Other Murder Sins

Paul also mentions – 'envyings, emulations, swellings, heresies', and conduct which is 'despiteful'. How do these come to be listed with the murder-hate family of sins? 'Envyings' and 'emulations' are translated from two Greek words, one meaning to burn or boil with strong feelings of jealousy and desire, and the other meaning to waste, ruin or deprive someone of what he possesses, obviously out of spite and ill-will. If I am an envious person, I will not be able to stand the thought that someone has a possession, a position or an opportunity which I lack. I will burn to have the same thing, and at the same time I will probably resent and despise the person who has advantages I lack. Obviously such an emotion will destroy any respect, affection or loyalty I may have toward that other person, and my spite and ill-will may even lead me to positively hurt or punish the other person ('relational murder'). The sins of backbiting and whispering mentioned earlier are often the outcome of petty jealousy.

By jealousy and fury Cain had already 'murdered' Abel in his heart well before he slew him, because his brother's offering was accepted and his own refused.

'Swellings' are manifestations of haughtiness, pride, or self-importance which put others down, withholding respect. 'Swellings' have a destructive, murderous element because the haughty people have no time or respect for anyone apart from themselves. They are often indifferent to Christian fellowship, unless it provides a platform for them to show their superiority, and they have no humble participation in teamwork for the Lord. Such things have long since been 'murdered' by the haughty heart.

The word 'despiteful' takes disdain even further, for the despiteful person not only holds others in contempt, but insults and injures them. We know also how a person who is conceited and consumed with his own ideas will soon surround himself with a circle of like-minded or admiring people to form a clique or party. This is what Paul means by 'heresies' – manifestations of 'party spirit'. Whatever they may pretend, such Christians do not truly submit to the authority of God's Word. They make up their own mind what they want, and are determined to get their way, and in getting it they will 'murder' and destroy anything and everything which frustrates or resists them, hurting people, churches and the very honour of Christ.

The Tongue – a Murder Weapon

Further proof that all these offences are members of the murder-hate family of sins comes in the letter of *James*, who tells us very plainly that the envying heart and the hostile tongue constitute deadly poison, giving rise to wars among believers in which they 'kill' one another. James is not speaking of literal murder, but like Paul, he recognises other branches of murder. In *James 3.8-9* and *14* we read: 'But the tongue can no man tame; it is an unruly evil, full of deadly poison *[which 'kills']*. Therewith bless we God, even the Father; and therewith curse we men, which are made after the similitude of God . . . But if ye have bitter envying and strife in your hearts, glory not, and lie not against the truth.'

James keeps up the theme in chapter *4.1-2:* 'From whence come wars and fightings among you? come they not hence, even of your lusts that war in your members? Ye lust, and have not: ye kill, and desire to have, and cannot obtain: ye fight and war, yet ye have not, because ye ask not.'

It is obvious that the church members addressed by James were not physically murdering each other, but they were doing so in their hearts and with their tongues, so James goes the whole way and charges them with moral murder. To repeat and summarise the position, any breach of relationships (without just, biblical cause) is a form of murder. Anyone who takes away the well-being or reputation of another, wilfully inflicting pain and hating that person from the heart, is a murderer. To reject other people as useless and to smash down their happiness, liberty, peace and purpose for living, is to morally kill them.

James explains it all in terms of war and peace. Conduct can either be characterised by war, hostility, fighting and killing (the murder-hate sins), or by peace and kindness. So he says – 'The wisdom that is from above is first pure, then peaceable, gentle, and easy to be intreated, full of mercy and good fruits, without partiality, and without hypocrisy. And the fruit of righteousness is sown in peace of them that make peace' *(James 3.17-18)*.

Murder of the Soul

There is still another form of murder which is even more terrible than anything so far mentioned, and yet this is also a form of murder in which true believers may possibly be implicated. The worst act of cruelty is the high crime of *spiritual* murder. Spiritual murder is included in the first statement of capital punishment in the Bible: 'Whoso sheddeth man's blood, by man shall his blood be shed: for in the image of God made he man' *(Genesis 9.6)*. In other words – it is because man has a soul that he is special, and elevated above the animals. For this reason alone human life is sacred. Because of the eternal soul, a man's death has eternal implications, for with death the period of probation on earth is instantly ended and the soul's eternal future is unchangeably resolved. The crime of physical murder includes the destruction of spiritual opportunity. The commandment – 'Thou shalt not kill' – covers the terminating of man's spiritual potential just as much as the life of his body. But what if we murder the soul while leaving the body alive?

The Lord Jesus spoke of this kind of murder – soul murder – when He told the Jews – 'Ye are of your father the devil, and the lusts of your father ye will do. He was a murderer from the beginning' *(John 8.44)*. When Satan brought about the fall of man, Adam and Eve did not immediately experience natural death, but on the day they ate the forbidden fruit they, and the entire human race with them, died *spiritually*, and thus in the Garden of Eden the devil became a murderer. Their physical death which occurred later was the *result* of their sin, but the essential act of murder was the temptation which led to their spiritual fall (as *Romans 5.12* makes clear).

Spiritual murder is likely to be committed whenever people are shut off from the Truth of God, or when soul-destroying error is taught. The Saviour condemned the Jewish teachers for taking away the key of knowledge, saying – 'Ye entered not in yourselves, and them that were entering in ye hindered' *(Luke 11.52)*.

The Lord uttered some of the severest words in the Bible when He warned against interfering with the spiritual opportunities of the young. He said to His disciples: 'It is impossible but that offences will come: but woe unto him, through whom they come! It were better for him that a millstone were hanged about his neck, and he cast into the sea, than that he should offend one of these little ones' *(Luke 17.1-2)*. There is no doubt that people will be held fully responsible for sins against the spiritual opportunities of others, and for any complicity in the murder of a soul. All militant atheists will stand guilty before God for this sin, and the scribes and the Pharisees of old will stand alongside them in that awful day, as will dignitaries of the Church of Rome and the arrogant exponents of theological liberalism. Every author of spiritual deadly poison will be punished for this grotesque crime – the murder of eternal souls.

Christians as Murderers?

But what about us? Is there any way in which believers may be guilty of this terrible crime? Certainly, because we may be spiritual murderers by refusing to save the lives of dying souls. Surely this was in the mind of the apostle Paul when he cried, 'Woe is unto me, if I preach not the gospel!' *(1 Corinthians 9.16.)* And this was also the thought behind Paul's words (recorded in *Acts 20.26-27*), 'Wherefore I take you to record this day, that I am pure from the blood of all men. For I have not shunned to declare unto you all the counsel of God.'

Have we been cowardly and silent when we should have told our family and acquaintances about the Lord and the way of salvation? Have we been cold and lazy over evangelism in our churches? Have preachers exhibited no inspiration or leadership to the people to be zealous and active in personal witness, district visitation, and Sunday School work? What about Bible-believing churches that have decided that they will not even attempt Sunday School work, or others which are happy to have a tiny, ill-supported effort? What are we doing with the saving light which we have?

On another level, do we wreck the credibility of our testimony by loose talk or unguarded episodes of ill-temper in our places of employment or study? Do we shock and dismay our children with hypocrisy and unsanctified conduct in the home? Do we injure the spiritual opportunities or progress of adults and children around us in any way? God forbid that we should find ourselves implicated in the tragedy of spiritual murder!

We must remember that viewed from a human standpoint souls are lost by a variety of causes. Some die from Gospel starvation, having received no spiritual sustenance from believers who lived next door, or who worked in the same place, or even through hearing no evangelistic preaching at church. Some die from suffocation because people who breathe the air of spiritual life have no compassion for them. Some perish from the poison of error, despite the fact that there were believers close by who could have put them right. And some are crushed and battered into confusion and doubt by the inconsistent lives of professing Christians – perhaps even parents.

'The Word of God is quick, and powerful, and sharper than any twoedged sword, piercing even to the dividing asunder of soul and spirit.' The sixth commandment is truly sifting and challenging to us all, whether a worldling or a child of God, for we have all been 'murderers' in some shape or form, and need the pardoning love of God, and the mighty power of the Spirit to enable us to live pure and pleasing lives for Him.

The Opposite of Murder

The opposite of murder-hate sinfulness is – unselfishness, affection, esteem, kindness, friendliness, helpfulness, supportiveness, encouragement and sympathy. These will never flourish until the battle against their opposite sins is taken seriously, by regular self-examination, repentance and effort not to re-offend. It helps greatly to hate these sins, seeing their destructive, murderous character. It also helps to pray much for other people, because this not only brings God's blessings into their lives, but it shapes our own attitude toward them, so that we desire the best for them, and cannot so easily despise them. It also helps, when hostile or disdainful thoughts arise, to remember our own sinful and foolish traits, and the extent to which we have benefited from the forgiveness and longsuffering of the Lord, as well as other people.

The murder-hostility family of sins is so deeply embedded in the fallen human heart that the spiritual warfare, and the sanctification process, is very largely taken up by this. Victory over these sins is the core of any advance in holiness, while to neglect this family is to lose the battle. Cultivation of the opposite positive virtues, by prayer, pleases the Lord, wins the lost, withstands all trials, and wonderfully sanctifies both church and family.

These opposite positive virtues are magnificently and supremely seen in the character of God, for He is love, and all the gracious virtues are continuous and unending in Him, and were gloriously revealed in the earthly life of Jesus Christ our Saviour and Lord. The substance of this commandment, both the negative and positive sides, is given in *Ephesians 4.31-32:*

> 'Let all bitterness, and wrath, and anger, and clamour, and evil speaking, be put away from you, with all malice: and be ye kind one to another, tenderhearted, forgiving one another, even as God for Christ's sake hath forgiven you.'

Abortion – Spearhead of Anti-Morality

Abortion is undoubtedly a form of murder, unless it is to save a mother's life. Tragically, most people today have been conditioned to think of it only as 'a terrible thing to have to do', and although it goes against every human instinct (except in the case of the most hard-hearted people) they do not realise that murder is involved. They do not grasp that foetal life is real life.

The day that abortion became legal in the UK in 1967 broke a kind of 'sound barrier' in the thinking of society, because God's most fundamental demands were no longer sacrosanct and respected. Man became his own lord and lawgiver, and the radical adaptation and rewriting of moral values became acceptable. Perhaps more than any other event, the legalisation of abortion, the brain-child of extreme and militant atheism, gave impetus to the permissive society, and caused people to relegate God and His laws to the 'benighted' past. But the Lord reigns, and the longing of believers is surely that expressed in a paraphrase of the tenth psalm –

> *Thou hast seen it, Lord, we know,*
> *Thou art King of all below.*
> *O, arise and lift Thy hand,*
> *Move in power towards this land;*
> *Break the mighty force of sin*
> *Bring a day of blessing in.*

[For serious study the author recommends the comprehensive chapter on abortion by John Jefferson Davis in his 1985 work, *Evangelical Ethics*, Baker Book House, Grand Rapids.]

7

The Seventh Commandment
'Thou shalt not commit adultery.'

One Fence to Disaster

'But fornication, and all uncleanness . . .
let it not be once named among you, as becometh saints.'
(Ephesians 5.3)

'THOU SHALT NOT commit adultery' is, of course, an absolute ban on physical fornication in all its forms, and it is certainly binding on all people in the literal sense. It passes the sentence of divine judgement on all improper sexual and sensual arousal and indulgence, together with all pornography and obscene speaking. Debauched, dissolute and licentious conduct all fall condemned under this holy commandment. Equally condemned is homosexual activity for sexual gratification, mental adultery and indecency. As for the producers of teen magazines inciting sensual adventure, wrecking the morals and real happiness of millions of young people, and also the producers of television soaps glamorising youth promiscuity, if they should face God at the end of life unforgiven and unconverted, their judgement will be decisive and terrible. Similarly public authorities, government ministers and teachers who implement the training of schoolchildren to believe that sexual indulgence is their right, as long as they are protected against conception will perish under this commandment. To spurn God's commandments, arrogantly substituting corrupt ideas, and teaching these to others, is to shake the fist of defiance at the Lord, and incur eternal punishment.

The use of the term *adultery* in the Bible shows that it has two departments – impurity and unfaithfulness. Many Christians are not aware that adultery is the chief of a family of sins which includes other forms of unfaithfulness, such as the betrayal of, or disloyalty to, any special bond or relationship to which we have a scriptural duty of faithfulness, especially our relationship with the Lord. The first half of this chapter will consider marital unfaithfulness, and its avoidance, while the second half will focus on unfaithfulness to our fellowship or friends, and also spiritual unfaithfulness.

For believers the 'faithfulness' aspect of this commandment is very protective, for it can save us from being plunged into misery and hurt; from throwing away priceless spiritual opportunities; from losing vital friendships; or from being tempted to leave the place or the church where God means us to be. The importance of 'harnessing' this rule positively in our Christian lives is immense, for it is designed to hold us safely within special bonds or relationships, marriage being the great example. Above all, it holds us in our loyalty to the Lord, keeping us from worldliness and from spiritual alliances with those who are not equally pledged to obey and love Him.

No commandment is merely an arbitrary, despotic demand from God, determined by unaccountable whim. If God forbids adultery, then we may be sure that there are a host of vital reasons, beginning with the fact that infinite purity and faithfulness are the essence of the glorious character of God.

Adultery – a Renouncing of Human Status

Proverbs 6.23-32 encourages us to look for the reasons behind this commandment. 'The commandment is a lamp,' says Solomon, 'and the law is light . . . Whoso committeth adultery with a woman lacketh understanding: he that doeth it destroyeth his own soul.' The adulterer does not care about the distinctive qualities of human nature. Physical adultery lowers people to the level of beasts in their subjection to appetites and lusts. A fundamental difference between human beings and animals is the gift of reason and the power of moral determination, by which self-control is exercised in personal, intimate relationships. Adultery is the renouncing of these distinctive human endowments, the renouncing of human status, and submission to animal urges and instincts. It is the despising and discarding of essential human dignity and worth.

Is it hard to avoid physical adultery? No, states the Bible, it is an easily avoidable and utterly unreasonable sin – especially in the case of believers in Christ. It involves setting aside that ordinary level of responsibility and moral strength which even worldlings may possess, and this is made clear from the firm tone of Paul's exhortation in *Ephesians 5.3* – 'But fornication, and all uncleanness . . . let it not be once named among you, as becometh saints.' Adultery is never a sudden fall, but always the result of entertaining lesser, but growing, wrong thoughts and unclean desires.

Self-Destructiveness of Adultery

Solomon's words quoted earlier warn that the adulterer destroys himself. Not only does adultery have a devastating effect on the one (or the family) who is betrayed, but on the adulterer personally. The Saviour warned (in *Matthew 12.39-45*) that it involves the entire moral collapse of the person concerned, unfaithfulness being a self-destructive force. He said – 'An evil and adulterous generation seeketh after a sign,' the words 'adulterous generation' being the key to what follows. Continuing, the Lord said: 'When the unclean spirit is gone out of a man, he walketh through dry places, seeking rest, and findeth none. Then he saith, I will return into my house from whence I came out; and when he is come, he findeth it empty, swept, and garnished. Then goeth he, and taketh with himself seven other spirits more wicked than himself, and they enter in and dwell there: and the last state of that man is worse than the first.' In this illustration the unclean spirit, the adulterous, unfaithful spirit, opens the door to a tremendous loss of character, and rapid decline into many other sins.

The many sins that are included in fornication begin with the despising and throwing out of human status and the betraying of a special relationship and trust made with binding promises. Other sins involved are deliberate lusting, selfishness, cruelty and deceitfulness. The old saying is true, that you can be a liar without being an adulterer, but you can't be an adulterer without also being a liar. No wonder the judgement passages of the Bible are so strong against adultery, such as where Paul says – 'Neither fornicators . . . nor adulterers . . . shall inherit the kingdom of God.' Peter also says – 'The Lord knoweth how to . . . reserve the unjust unto the day of judgment to be punished: but chiefly them that walk after the flesh in the lust of uncleanness, and despise government [God's authority].' God will, of course, judge all sin, but there are 'magnet' sins which gather up numerous other sins, and these acts are marked out for particular severity. Adultery is in this category, for – 'whoremongers and adulterers God will judge.' The same is true of all forms of sexual indulgence, whether in thought or action, because all are self-destructive, for character and spiritual life.

Obviously we are most likely to recoil from any temptation to unfaithfulness or sensual imaginings and activities if we have an adequate grasp of the vileness of these things. The mind needs to be equipped with a realistic sense of repugnance over such sins. In this sense 'the commandment is a lamp', because it reveals the reasons for the prohibition of the sin. It is also a lamp which keeps the night traveller on the track, preventing him from getting into dangerous terrain.

Preventive Remedies to Adultery

To change the analogy, this commandment is a kind of safety fence or boundary which must never be crossed in any circumstances. In any marital dissatisfaction or argument, there is a certain fence we will never cross; a line over which we will not go. The forbidden territory starts at the point where the fallen and wretched human heart begins to murmur against or to question a God-given union, perhaps to resent or regret that relationship and wish for something else. Should that 'no-man's land' be approached, and should disgraceful ideas be hurled into our minds by the devil, we will then find ourselves confronted by a high fence inscribed with the words – 'Thou shalt not even think of unfaithfulness!' If the weakness of the flesh with its selfishness, insensitivity, ill-temper and ill-nature causes a husband and wife to fall into a bad relationship, they will be protected from their worst behaviour by this boundary line – if they fear God and respect His Commandments. Only defiant fools will climb over this barrier and press on, allowing forbidden ideas to ferment, destroying the apparatus of faithfulness, and yielding to burning thoughts of hostility, resentment or self-pity. The basis of all loyalty and faithfulness is to respect, value, honour, and even fear that fence, which limits the progress of bad thoughts, and prevents problems from getting beyond control. God has given us this boundary for our vital protection, and only conceit and wilful carnality abuses it.

We must maintain a firm determination to quench and bring under control the earliest thought of murmuring against the precious relationship which God has ordained, enacted, sealed and sanctified. Married people must fear the sin of abusing God's protective, containing boundary, for they belong to each other, and to wish otherwise is unthinkable. None dare go into that no-man's land to contemplate how things might be with someone else, or to harbour hatreds, because to question the special relationship of marriage even in thought is already an act of betrayal and 'adultery'.

Adultery begins as soon as God's barrier is doubted and despised. Once more we note Paul's words – 'Fornication, and all uncleanness . . . let it not be once named among you.' How can husbands and wives be sure to avoid temptations to unfaithfulness? First, we are to love one another. Secondly, we are to thank God for each other, and pray for each other daily. Thirdly, we must never cross the boundary of the seventh commandment to even entertain ideas of being better off without each other. Hostile or resentful or self-pitying thoughts must be expelled from the mind immediately they arise, and substituted with appreciative thoughts and recollections.

Fourthly, we are not to weaken ourselves by surrendering to the desires of the flesh in other areas of our lives, such as self-pampering covetousness. It may be that a husband and wife have a very affectionate relationship and have never been tempted to unfaithfulness, but they give way to covetousness with no attempt at self-control, and pamper themselves with entertainment, eating, creature comforts, clothes, or possessions. People sometimes come to the point where they must satisfy every whim and desire. These pursuits may not be immoral, but excessive self-indulgence is always a surrender to Satan and the flesh, leading to a considerable weakening of character. Before long the tempter may move to marital temptations, minor disharmony at first, then building up to greater temptations. The weakened person is the most vulnerable.

Some believers watch hours of television entertainment, award themselves extravagant holidays, and justify and buy whatever possessions they like. But in so doing they virtually offer their throats to the enemy of their souls, and may soon be taken captive by him at his will. When the muscles of self-denial are emaciated beyond use, then Satan moves to do whatever he wants. If adultery should be his choice, then he will almost effortlessly push a believer first into that no-man's land of entertaining unfaithful thoughts, and from there into passionate lusting, and finally into fleshly sin.

Some believers are so foolish (and sinful) as to look admiringly at the opposite sex (or at pictures), allowing their minds to derive emotional and sexual excitement, and so committing the sins of fornication or adultery in their minds. The warning of the Saviour is well known – 'Whosoever looketh on a woman to lust after her hath committed adultery with her already in his heart.' 'This is the will of God,' says Paul, 'even your sanctification, that ye should abstain from fornication: that every one of you should know how to possess his vessel in sanctification and honour; not in the lust of concupiscence [longing], even as the Gentiles which know not God' (1 Thessalonians 4.3-5).

Within marriage, love must be kept alive, but some men are very deficient in *expressing* love for their wives. Marital love, in the Bible, includes honour, esteem, respect, gentleness, courtesy, and affection, and these should be cultivated, treasured and deepened.

Loyalty to Fellow Believers

Adultery, we remember, is the representative sin of a whole family of unfaithful deeds and attitudes, and we turn now to the subject of fellowship between believers to see how the seventh commandment preserves close and blessed ties. Admittedly we are not bound to our spiritual brothers and sisters by the same absolute and unbreakable ties which join us to the Lord and His Word, or which join us in marriage, yet we are nevertheless linked in loyalty to each other by scriptural commands and obligations. What help do we get from the seventh commandment to maintain our friendships and also our team-partnerships in various spheres of Christian service? What when difficulties arise, and personalities clash? What when stresses and workloads lead to misunderstandings and unworthy quarrels or ill-feeling? How can we protect ourselves from matters getting out of hand and leading to alienation with all its spiritual damage?

In all cases there is a duty of mutual respect and loyalty to the bond of church membership, or to any friendship which God has graciously given, unless there are serious problems such as unrepented-of sin, or repudiation of sound doctrine. Let the seventh commandment be seen as a high wall round every Christian friendship or relationship, and let the inscription read: 'You shall not be unfaithful to your spiritual family, friends, and fellow-labourers in the Lord.' Then when troubles arise we shall say to ourselves: 'Thus far, and no further!'

Satan may try to influence us, saying, 'You could do better without this person! Detest him! Resent her! Despise him! Avoid her! Speak against him! Ignore her! Tell others about his defects! Upset her! Bait him! Change your friends! Change your circle!' With the influence of the principle taught in the seventh commandment, all such ideas will be rejected for what they are, the appealings of Satan to our residual sin-nature. We will then look to God to garrison our hearts and minds, keeping us from foolish sin.

If a professing Christian is unnecessarily disloyal to his local church (assuming that the church is sound and striving to obey the Lord), he betrays a solemn and special relationship ordained by God. A person who is critical, scheming or obstructive to the gathered church of Christ is guilty in God's sight of unfaithfulness to the body of Christ.

Faithfulness is a very precious and highly protective virtue which flows from the very heart of our faithful, patient, covenant-keeping God. It will keep us in the way of blessing, enlarge our usefulness and bring us limitless happiness and joy, whether in marriage, among friends, or in Christian service. Team service especially depends upon strong and patient mutual faithfulness.

The Cultivation of Loyalty

It is not surprising that when Paul pleaded that help be given to Euodias and Syntyche, so that they should be of the same mind in the Lord, he followed that by saying – 'Let your moderation be known unto all men' *(Philippians 4.5)*. It has been said that the Greek word translated *moderation* in the King James Version could well be seen as a combination of the following virtues: forbearance, yieldedness, geniality, kindliness, gentleness, sweet reasonableness, considerateness, charitableness, mildness, magnanimity, and generosity.

Large-heartedness has been suggested as another good single-word translation. This is both the preventive and healing medicine which limits and extinguishes mutual hostility and suspicion between friends. But if the preventive virtue fails, then we must be held safe by the boundary fence which stops any failure of relationships from getting out of hand. The words, 'Thou shalt not . . . ' must curb the unworthy tendencies of fallen hearts. Do we practise this? Have we firmly resolved never to entertain extreme thoughts and destructive hatreds in all our sanctified relationships? What a help to us these commandments are when rightly used! Truly Lord, 'Thy commandment is exceeding broad'! *(Psalm 119.96.)*

Going back almost thirty years (well out of reach of public recollection or identification) the writer remembers two elderly ladies in his church fellowship who were quite unlike the majority, because they had a nose for anything that was less than perfect. Armed with acute analytical powers, they saw – or thought they saw – ulterior motives and bad attitudes in everyone, especially young people. They had their own mental classification of people, dividing them into passable and untrustworthy groupings, and little escaped their critical view. In vain one tried to persuade them that when problems are perceived, intercession is the mouthpiece of faithfulness. They had become utterly negative in their constant practice of putting the worst possible construction on every human situation in the church, and their outlook and thinking was beyond healing.

Scripture would call them busybodies in other people's lives, and meddlers, even though they never directly challenged their targeted 'offenders'. This is a sinful and tragic state to get into. If 'negativism' and suspicion begin to take hold of our minds (and the devil will sometimes try to bring this about) and we find ourselves acting as investigator, judge and jury in making assessments of others, then we must repent, stop that train of thought, and remember our duty of faithfulness to each other. Offences will arise, but not on the scale suspected by the negative thinker, who eventually functions more like a soap scriptwriter than a believer in the life-transforming power and grace of God. The Lord is wonderfully faithful, and so we have the seventh commandment, for which the positive virtues are loyalty, magnanimity, thinking no evil, rejoicing not in iniquity, hoping all things, and love that never fails.

Negative policing of the church fellowship is usually grossly inaccurate and unfair, and always involves sinful gossip, even if this is clothed in pious concern and shared only with a few confidants. May we value and pursue the great and scriptural rules of fellowship. Faithfulness and loyalty to God, and to spouse, then, on another plane to fellow believers in our church fellowship and to friends, is both a duty and a reflection of the very heart of God, and we must guard it and develop it to His delight and glory.

What is Spiritual Adultery?

In various Old Testament passages (examples are set out in the chart overleaf) Israel and Judah are charged with the sin of adultery through worshipping pagan idols. Frequent application of the seventh commandment to *spiritual* adultery in both Testaments leaves us in no doubt that we should make this important connection today. Apostasy from the Truth is described as adultery because it abandons our total and exclusive commitment to the Lord and His Word by associating with false religious ideas, or with worldliness. It is important to note that when the Israelites committed spiritual adultery, they did not usually renounce the true religion, but introduced pagan worship alongside it. Spiritual adultery today is the adultery of a double life, in which believers maintain evangelical worship, and serve the world at the same time.

To bring this matter more sharply into focus we must emphasise that the Jews of old enjoyed the benefits of a national covenant with Almighty God. Any defection on their part was a betrayal or breach of a unique and solemn relationship, and this is what made their spiritual whoredom a matter of adultery. We too, as redeemed people today, have a covenant relationship with the Lord, through Christ, and any breach of this is spiritual adultery. All the pain and loss suffered by British evangelicalism over the last hundred years has been the direct result of unfaithfulness on the part of many ministers, and others, who have led God's people into compromise with false teachers. Yet the encouragement of ecumenical alliances and unsound literature continues. There is a fence which bears in letters of blood the seventh commandment in New Testament language, and it reads:

> 'Be ye not unequally yoked together with unbelievers: for what fellowship hath righteousness with unrighteousness? and what communion hath light with darkness? and what concord hath

Christ with Belial? or what part hath he that believeth with an infidel? and what agreement hath the temple of God with idols? for ye are the temple of the living God; as God hath said, I will dwell in them, and walk in them; and I will be their God, and they shall be my people. Wherefore come out from among them, and be ye separate, saith the Lord, and touch not the unclean thing; and I will receive you' *(2 Corinthians 6.14-17)*.

To enter into spiritual alliances with the Lord's enemies is, viewed biblically, an act of adultery – even treachery.

Examples of Old Testament applications of adultery to the *spiritual* adultery of idol worship

Isaiah charges the people with adultery for 'enflaming your-selves with idols under every green tree' *(Isaiah 57.3-5)*.

Jeremiah says that the land 'committed adultery with stones and with stocks' *(Jeremiah 3.8-9)*. He also condemns the 'adultery' of burning incense to Baal *(Jeremiah 7.9)*.

He calls the people adulterers for not being 'valiant for the truth' *(Jeremiah 9.2-3)*.

He refers to their adulteries in trusting in falsehood, and mentions the 'lewdness of thy whoredom . . . in the fields' – where the idol shrines were built *(Jeremiah 13.25 and 27)*.

He says the land was full of adulterers, both prophet and priest compromising because they 'prophesied in Baal', causing the people to err *(Jeremiah 23.10-14)*.

Ezekiel also charges the nations with idolatry, adding, 'with their idols have they committed adultery' *(Ezekiel 23.37)*.

Hosea is told by God to love an adulteress to illustrate 'the love of the Lord toward the children of Israel, who look to other gods' *(Hosea 3.1)*.

Malachi speaks of the abomination of Judah in forsaking the love of the Lord and marrying 'the daughter of a strange god' *(Malachi 2.11)*.

Do not commit adultery must be the sign on the fence that separates us from the error and unbelief of false spiritual teaching, including reading the books of those who offend the Lord by their compromise, or from going to Bible colleges where the Word of God is not loved and respected, or from other similarly unfaithful and harmful activities. These are serious matters, so serious that a fundamental moral commandment is assigned to them.

But spiritual adultery is also committed when irreligious worldly delights are welcomed wholesale into the lives or into the worship of the Lord's people, for James says –

> 'Ye adulterers and adulteresses, know ye not that the friendship of the world is enmity with God? whosoever therefore will be a friend of the world is the enemy of God . . . Purify your hearts, ye double minded' *(James 4.4 and 8)*.

Any Christian believer who becomes a lover of the things of this world – its entertainments, delights and fashions – becomes also an adulterer. He crosses the fence of the seventh commandment to draw his pleasure from a culture which is against God, and in so doing he offends and hurts his God, becoming guilty of spiritual disloyalty. When we allow our tastes to be conditioned to appreciate music and entertainment linked with a debauched, sinful and worldly philosophy of life, we place ourselves on the slope to inevitable spiritual adultery. In no time we find ourselves increasingly infatuated with things condemned in Scripture, and wholly inconsistent with a Christian profession. Our witness then becomes hypocritical and offensive to God, for how can we call lost sinners out of Vanity Fair if we ourselves are intoxicated by its delights? The text we have already quoted should be taken far more seriously than it often is – 'Know ye not that the friendship of the world is enmity with God?' The adulterer (in the usage of James) is a person who desires the things of this world alongside spiritual blessings. The great commandment against unfaithfulness must form a clear line over which we will not step; a boundary to keep us faithful to the Lord.

The opposite positive virtues of adultery are purity and faithfulness, in sexual conduct, in marriage, in other human relationships, and in spiritual matters, and for these virtues we strive, remembering again that graphic and striking expression given by the Spirit to the apostle Paul – 'That every one of you should know how to possess his vessel in sanctification and honour' *(1 Thessalonians 4.4)*.

8

The Eighth Commandment
'Thou shalt not steal.'

The Many Faces of Theft

'Let him that stole steal no more: but rather let him
labour . . . that he may have to give to him that needeth.'
(Ephesians 4.28)

ARE THERE any thieves reading these words? Is anyone a persistent thief? The writer remembers seeing a rather jolting poster mounted on a pillar in a supermarket in a district notorious for its high crime rate. In lurid red letters the poster read simply – 'Shoplifting is stealing!' Did the management really think that such an obvious fact needed to be spelled out? Evidently they did, and they were probably right. They knew that for many people the act of taking a few items from a vastly wealthy firm does not feel like stealing at all. Perhaps similar shock-tactics are needed even for born-again Christians, because, according to Scripture, there is the heart of a thief surviving within every one of us. We do many things which in God's sight are nothing other than crimes of theft, and we need to be reminded of the full scope of the eighth commandment.

If posters about theft were put up in our churches, one might pro-claim, 'Excessive leisure is stealing!' Another might read: 'To be uninvolved in Christian service is stealing!' Many such posters would be needed to cover the numerous acts of unconscious theft carried out every day in the spiritual sphere by God's people, because (or so pastors often complain) this kind of theft is so com-mon that Christians do not feel that it is wrong. Surely then, if we really want to please the Lord and to be blessed with progress in our spiritual lives, we will be keen to identify the many faces of theft, and then to mortify all our stealing ways.

The commandment – 'Thou shalt not steal' – covers a great family of depriving and defrauding sins. In this chapter we shall chiefly apply this commandment to believers. As we have said, it is an act of theft for believers to help themselves to excessive leisure at the expense of their fellow believers, who are denied their help and commitment in the work of the church. Mr and Mrs Uncommitted are thieves if they leave it to others to bear the brunt of the church expenses and the manning of church activities, while they spend most of their time and money on themselves. They may speak much about their love of the doctrines of grace, and of the Lord's dealings with them, but in God's sight they are passengers at best and thieves at worst. One day – perhaps by way of severe chastisement – they may feel the weight of God's warning to those who defraud their fellow believers – 'the Lord is the avenger of all such' *(1 Thess-alonians 4.6).*

Stealing is a Compound Sin

Before we look in detail at the various ways in which we, even as Christian people, may be thieves, we need to recharge our minds with a keen awareness of the unusually base nature of stealing. Theft in all its forms is particularly low and unpleasant because it is saturated with pride, deceit and hypocrisy. In the secular sphere, arrogance is seen in the way a thief suspends the basic rules of society and exempts himself from them. Common thieves, or the perpetrators of fraud in business life, would not want anything to be stolen from *them*. Like everyone else, they want law and order to be maintained in society, and would be appalled if *their* children were mugged or *their* homes burgled. Yet when they swindle or steal they exempt themselves from the law which they expect to be maintained for their own comfort and protection. They suspend the rules of society for their own activities, and there is no higher level of arrogance and selfishness than this.

Coming back to the uncommitted church member who steals by withholding his stewardship and effort from the church, this person would be greatly put out if he ever found himself overburdened because of the indolence of others. All forms of stealing are arrogant, making the offenders regard themselves as uniquely above the rules which they expect everyone else to follow. Mr and Mrs Uncommitted, who keep for themselves their due proportion of time, energy and resources, often have a very puffed up view of themselves. They imagine they are a superior class of people who are somehow entitled to have a much better car, more leisure time, an unusually beautiful home, or the right to spend many weeks away on super holidays, and so on. They are *special* people, and do not feel they have to justify their theft.

Stealing is also callous because the thief does not care about the effect of his crime upon the person who is deprived. The extortioner who charges excessive rents does not care what hardship he causes, and the person who sells a defective car does not care what trouble his fraud may cause the buyer. It is the same with uncommitted Christians in a church, because they do not care how their spiritual laziness imposes on the lives of others. Stealing is always heartless.

Stealing from God

1. Stealing commitment

What exactly happens when Christians steal their time and resources from their church? God brings His people together in congregations and distributes among them gifts and abilities for Christian service. At the same time, He assigns to each congregation a workload which includes evangelistic, teaching and caring ministries to both adults and children. Let us suppose that half the members of any congregation choose to take only a superficial interest in these ministries, and do not pull their weight at all. When not super-advancing their careers, they spend their evenings at home occupied in various relaxations and making improvements about the house. They paint things more often than necessary, and give themselves to making various rooms as perfect as they could possibly be. In the summer months they produce exceptionally beautiful gardens or set their energies to quite a full programme of enjoyable entertaining of old friends, or to other leisure pursuits.

If single Christians engage in excessive fun-based fellowship, groups going hither and thither, dining out, even flying off on holiday jaunts, they will inevitably be applying time, energy and resources to these pursuits effectively stolen from believers who work hard in the mission of the church. Some of the latter are so busy that they can scarcely spend any time at home looking after their families, and the lazy ones (the thieves) may even speak critically of their neglect of their families. This form of theft is amazingly common in churches in the affluent West.

Numerous professing Christians are living as though the following prayer would suit them very well:– 'I thank Thee, Lord, for saving my soul! I thank Thee for suffering and dying for all my sin on Calvary. Now that I am a Christian and I am going to Heaven, I love to sing praises and listen to fine sermons. I also thank Thee Lord for the Christian liberty which enables me to avoid any meaningful commitment to Christian service, and to run my life and spend my free time just as I want to.' The reality is, the offenders are thieves, even if consciences have been rendered inoperative by the widespread acceptance of 'ease' in Zion. We must long to see a return to the zeal of former times in our churches, for the work of the Gospel, the glory of our Saviour, and also for the true fulfilment, assurance and blessedness of individual believers.

2. Stealing the benefits of fellowship

Another form of stealing from the community of believers occurs when we fail to contribute what is due in interpersonal relations, friendship, prayerful helpfulness to others, hospitality, encouragement, and sympathy. A debit balance caused by coldness, aloofness, no give and all take, is another form of theft, for we all owe a contribution of effort to promote fellowship and helpfulness to other people in our church. As Christians we have a debt and a duty to help build relationships and to care for one another to the glory of God. Sadly, some believers are happy to take the benefits of Christian fellowship without putting anything in, and we need to ask ourselves – Is this true of me? Perhaps I do not go out of my way to be a blessing to others or to take a supportive interest in their circumstances. Many are very kind to me, but I do not go out of my way to plan acts of kindness to them. Perhaps other people are very patient with us, bearing with our many failings, mistakes, and offences, but if anyone upsets us, we, in our turn, refuse to exercise any patience and forgiveness towards them. If a balance sheet could be drawn up showing all the benefits we have received alongside those which we have given, would we be revealed as heavily in debt to the church community? And if so, are we happy to go on living like this year after year, taking much, but seldom giving?

Perhaps we take the ministry, but disdain the life of the congregation. We like to be in the company of those who are always warm and cheerful; who look on the bright side and never fail to encourage us or even make us laugh, but as for ourselves – are we always gloomy, critical and long-faced? Is the balance sheet unsatisfactory here too? And do we take the 'social' benefits, but show no supportive appreciation of the spiritual purpose and objectives of our church?

As one looks back over the years, one thinks of many people who have taken up a great amount of 'pastoral time'. To mention this is to tread on delicate ground because we do not want to deter people from seeking advice and help whenever they need it, nevertheless one cannot help remembering people who absorbed hours and hours of encouragement and kindness from many 'shepherds' within the church, and then ended up as disappointments to all. After all the investment of time, attention and concern, what did the balance sheet look like? Did the people who received so much help proceed to give anything back? Or did they eventually go on their way ungrateful and critical? Some balance sheets show a story of daylight robbery. All of us experience problems and need the help and support of the fellowship at some time, but when the Lord blesses us, what do we then give in return for our spiritual 'hospitalisation'?

3. Stealing within marriage

Another form of stealing in the sphere of relationships occurs in the unique union of marriage, already touched on in a previous chapter. There is a very telling passage in *1 Corinthians 7.3-5* where Paul says –

> 'Let the husband render unto the wife due benevolence: and likewise also the wife unto the husband. The wife hath not power of her own body, but the husband: and likewise also the husband

hath not power of his own body, but the wife. Defraud ye not one the other . . . '

This text should not be limited to the subject of intimate relations, for the first part speaks broadly of 'due benevolence'. In Christian marriage there is obviously a mutual debt of love, affection and understanding. Do husbands and wives honour their obligations, or do they deprive each other? If they hold back 'due benevolence', Paul calls it *fraud*, or a breach of the eighth commandment. One has cheated the other out of due love and affection, care and attention, encouragement and support, and perhaps many other duties beside.

Some professing Christians have been burdensome and unaffectionate partners, stealing the happiness, youth and years from the other party, along with many hopes and dreams, and giving nothing. If we fall short in the rendering of 'due benevolence' it is never too late to seek the help of God for a new – even if late – chapter of married life, for the Lord is wonderfully forgiving and kind.

4. Stealing God's lordship

Unsaved people steal from God all the time, taking their lives, gifts, health, strength and years, and spending them all on themselves. However, it needs to be repeated that converted people may also be guilty of stealing from God. Some steal *headship* from Him, clinging on to self-determination. They say that Jesus owns them; that they are not their own; that they are bought with a price; and that He is their Lord and Master, yet they steal the right to determine where they shall be employed next year, what they shall study, what they will do with their lives, and where they shall establish their homes. They steal the right to make great personal decisions without reference to the Lord, or the Word. Sometimes they speak of seeking guidance, but as soon as they want something badly enough, they just go ahead and do it or buy it. Some flit about guided entirely by impulses and whims. Do we steal the government of our lives from Almighty God, or do we sincerely seek to find His will in all the major twists and turns of life?*

We have heard of believing middle-aged couples with older teenage children, whose chief purpose in supporting a particular church was to place their children in a safe (and good class) environment where they would hopefully marry 'acceptable' partners. Such parents, it appears, have left churches located in poorer areas, lacking large teenage groups of the 'right' kind, in order to attend churches better located and endowed. We have heard of people in their forties and fifties who have been prepared to jettison all their claimed doctrinal convictions to support the kind of church they would previously have strongly criticised, in order to get a material safe haven for their children. Inner city mission churches often find themselves stripped of such adult believers who want a church more comfortable for themselves and 'suitable' for their youngsters. But does this not show a lack of spirituality and faith? Does it indicate love for the Truth, zeal for evangelism and dedication to God, or believers only concerned to take what they want?

5. Stealing salvation blessings

How many Christian people 'steal' even their spiritual blessings? The Jews did this in Old Testament days, and it was one of the reasons why they were finally rejected by God. Their crime was that they seized their blessings as their exclusive property. They were supposed to represent the message of God's Word and ways to the world, but they took the view that God's message and Temple were exclusively for them, for they were the nation of God, and Gentiles were mere dogs and beyond hope. As Christian believers we have not been saved solely to listen to the Word and be thrilled in our

---

* See *Steps for Guidance,* Peter Masters, Wakeman Trust, London.

own souls. We have to challenge ourselves with a number of questions. Have I been blessed by the Lord for my sake alone? Do I keep this for myself, or do I pass it on? Am I a witnessing believer? Do I give away literature or tapes? Do I invite the lost to services? Do I teach Sunday School children, and visit to recruit others? Or am I like those Jews of old who said, 'This is all for us'?

To be selfish in these matters is a form of stealing, because God has made it so very clear to us that we are to be stewards and distributors of benefits. Has selfishness, laziness, cowardice or lovelessness driven us to steal from God? How many believers who would never dream of committing shoplifting or burglary, steal the most priceless things of all from the Lord, keeping them for themselves? Is it not stealing for oneself the greatest treasure of compassion in the history of the world?

6. Stealing our own possessions

We also steal if we regard our *material* blessings as our very own property. Another great sin of the Jews was their attitude to their land, and this should serve as a warning for us in our day. God gave them a very large tract of country, and they occupied it, but the Lord had expressly told them that all the ground was His *(Exodus 19.5)*. He taught them that they were the custodians rather than the owners of the land, and that they did not have the right to sell any part of it permanently, only to lease it short-term, so that it would at length revert to the original custodian. *Leviticus 25.23* records this command: 'The land shall not be sold for ever: for the land is mine; for ye are strangers and sojourners with me.'

They were tenants; occupants; visitors; lodgers, but not owners, God alone being the freeholder. Jews who were truly spiritual – the born-again minority of the Old Testament community – understood this very well. In *1 Chronicles*, we read a wonderful prayer of David, who said to the Lord, 'For we are strangers before thee, and sojourners *[tenants]*, as were all our fathers: our days on the earth are as a shadow.'

David utters the same sentiment in *Psalm 39* – 'for I am a stranger with thee, and a sojourner'. However, by and large, the Jews regarded the land as their own property, and they do so to this day. The truly converted and enlightened Jew knew that God's promise of land referred ultimately to a future possession of glorified land in the eternal realm.

The application for us today is that everything we possess really belongs to God, and we are only stewards and custodians. In a sense a true Christian does not own anything, for he has said to God, 'I am not my own; I am bought with a price.' One of the worst mistakes we can make is to puff out the chest and say, 'This is my house! This is my car!' Believers should never indulge in feelings of possessive gratification, revelling in ownership, basking in the sense of things possessed. To derive any satisfaction or sense of achievement by indulging the emotions of ownership is a very damaging influence on the soul, for it spoils true consecration and stewardship, and causes us to 'steal' from the Lord.

The only acceptable standard for believers is to acknowledge to God that we are only custodians and stewards, and to pledge ourselves to the faithful 'administration' of all our possessions. In saying this we are straying into the territory of the tenth commandment, but our purpose is only to show that all our possessions must be at God's disposal all the time. We are to be hospitable and to lend our facilities within the household of faith. We are to be ready to sell things, if necessary, to raise funds for a great spiritual objective, perhaps, or because something we possess is a bad example or an offence to others. To be jealously possessive is to steal from the Lord our Redeemer. We say to God –

> *Take myself, and I will be,*
> *Ever, only, all for Thee.*

Literal Theft by Believers

But what about literal theft? Are believers guilty of this? In *Ephesians 4.28* Paul gives a rather startling exhortation when he says to church members – 'Let him that stole steal no more.' Perhaps the apostle has in mind not the one-time 'professional' crook who has since been converted, but the active sponger among the Lord's people. In those days many slaves were converted and some of these may have felt that they had a right to steal. We sympathise with those who were owned by others and knew what it was to be abused and taken advantage of. They received minimal wages, often nothing at all, and they thought that a little pilfering was almost the least of their rights. But once they were converted they had to steadfastly resist any temptation to pilfer, no matter how much their owners took advantage of them.

Today we may well have those who steal or commit fraud in our congregations even though there is not even that marginal excuse of being downtrodden slaves. I remember the case of a successful businessman who was secretly proud of the way he could dress up goods and sell them for much more than they were worth, yet he was a respected Christian believer. When people have committed fraud on a regular basis before their conversion, they sometimes slip back into the same practices.

I remember also the case of a Christian salesman who had swindled his company for years by making inflated expense claims. Apparently everyone else in his office did it and he would have been unpopular if he had not made out claims similar to those of his colleagues. One day the Spirit of God touched his heart and he was deeply convicted of his sinfulness over many years. There may be many other Christians overcharging and fiddling books, but God forbids it absolutely.

What is the opposite positive virtue? We are to be a *giving* people, as Paul says in *Ephesians 4.28,* 'Let him that stole steal no more: but rather let him labour . . . that he may have to give to him that needeth' – and to the Lord's work. Do we rob God? Do we polish and paint, beautify or delight in the things which we claim as our own? Are we 'thieves', hoping that no one – not even the Lord – will notice? Let our philosophy be to give all to the Lord. Let us say, 'Everything I have is Christ's and I am a tenant here, a steward. Nothing that I have is my own.'

When we read the eighth commandment, let us read into it the kindly, pleading tones of the Lord we love, speaking in the same manner as when He said to Peter, 'Lovest thou me?' May we hear the voice of our Saviour in the words – 'Thou shalt not steal' – so that He seems to say, 'Would you steal from Me?' How can we steal in any form from Him, our divine and dearest Friend? And let us also hear in these words the opposite positive exhortation that flows directly from the character of God, the eternal Giver, 'Thou shalt be a great giver and succourer, giving the Gospel, your love, your intercessory prayer, yourself, and your means, to the cause of Christ.'

9

The Ninth Commandment
'Thou shalt not bear false witness.'

A Family of Lies

'Lie not one to another, seeing that ye have put off the old man
with his deeds; and have put on the new man . . . '
(Colossians 3.9-10)

TO TITUS, Paul spoke of – 'God, that cannot lie' – a statement as magnificent as it is simple. God is no mirage or product of human fiction, nor does He change with the times or adapt His being to shifting circumstances. All His statements are perfect and true, for God is Truth, in every sense of the word. Men and women, by contrast, are never what they seem. Everyone's outward manner hides a multitude of weaknesses and sinful ways, but the Lord is everything the Bible says He is.

God is also truthful in the sense that He is never mistaken. Our statements are often wrong not because we are lying, but because we are ignorant of the facts, but God can never be mistaken because His infinite knowledge and wisdom complements His truthfulness. It is a great comfort to remember that God's promises are founded upon this combination of divine attributes. While our undertakings are subject to unseen future developments, God's are made in the light of His perfect knowledge, and will never fail.

There is another immensely comforting thought about God's truthfulness, namely that it represents all 'departments' of His infinite being. When God says a thing, He means it deeply. He does not make clinically correct pronouncements like a human academic or politician who may lack feeling. God's words spring from the whole of His infinite being. We so often say things which are truthful, but our hearts are not in what we say. We may, for example, give an unspecific invitation to someone to visit us, when we only partly mean it. Perhaps we are tired or short of time, and, on balance, would be rather relieved if the person proved unable to come. We are reasonably sincere, but not wholly genuine in what we say. But when God makes His effectual call to lost souls He means it with the whole of His mighty heart of love.

Many years ago two leading political figures of the same party fell into dispute, one calling the other a 'desiccated calculating machine'. The words were said acrimoniously, but contained an acknowledgement that the one insulted was a brilliant economist. The complaint was that he lacked compassion or feeling or heart, something that could never be said about Almighty God. The salvation which He designed is no mere technical solution to the problem of sin, it is an expression of His great love toward the elect. When God, in Christ, bids us come to Himself, He does so out of deep compassion and incomprehensible tenderness, being truthful with all His mighty being.

As we consider the ninth commandment we must begin by recognising the infinite integrity of our God, Who hates all falsehood, and Who loves truth. As believers we have been washed from all past deceitfulness, and adopted into the family of truthfulness and genuineness. Our calling is to hold truth in the highest regard, and to dedicate ourselves to the work of developing and maintaining a truthful spirit in every aspect of life.

More than Defamation

A casual reader may think that this ninth commandment refers solely to defamation of character, but a brief look at the meaning of the words quickly shows a much broader meaning. The Hebrew word translated *bear* ('Thou shalt not BEAR false witness') means – *look upon, consider, pay heed to, listen to.* It can also mean *give* or *communicate.* The commandment not only prohibits the hearing of (knowingly), and the utterance of, false testimony, it prohibits having anything at all to do with false testimony. We may paraphrase it in this way: 'You shall not invent, or give your attention to, or think about, or pass on false witness.' We must neither be a giver or receiver of it.

To express it another way, the commandment says – 'You shall not carry false witness either in your head, in your heart, or on your lips.' It is a breach of this commandment even to fuel one's own mind with exaggerated or imagined ideas about another person's faults, because we are then *bearing* (carrying and considering) false witness even though these defamatory thoughts may never pass our lips in gossip.

What exactly is 'false witness'? It is any dishonest version of events, or any untrue statement. It may be gossip or slander against someone, or it may be untrue information about oneself, to impress others. It includes phoney or overstretched excuses concocted to get one out of trouble or disgrace. Even unrealistic flattery is a lie, and harmful because it gives a person a false view of himself, possibly producing pride. Parents have often ruined their children with unfounded flattery.

The King James translation certainly suggests that the falsehood must be '*against* thy neighbour', but the Hebrew word translated *against* is very elastic, and equally means 'with or touching thy neighbour'.

The old writers did full justice to the broad compass of this commandment as we see from Matthew Henry, who wrote: 'The ninth commandment concerns our own and our neighbour's good name. This commandment forbids, (1) Speaking falsely in any matter, lying, equivocating, and in any way devising and designing to deceive our neighbour. (2) Speaking unjustly against our neighbour. (3) Bearing false witness against him . . . slandering, backbiting, tale-bearing, aggravating what is done amiss and making it worse than it is, and in any way endeavouring to raise our own reputation upon the ruin of our neighbour's.'

Harmful and Ugly Aspects of a Lie

The first alarming aspect of a lie for a believer is that the Holy God on Whom we depend for all our well-being and assurance will turn His face and His gracious smile away from the liar, the indwelling Holy Spirit being grieved (according to the warning of *Ephesians 4.29-30*). What a foolish thing, to cut ourselves off from the blessing of our God by a lie!

The second alarming aspect of a lie is the betrayal of human trust. The person to whom the lie is spoken is betrayed, for that person has extended to the liar the compliment of trust, belief and respect, listening to him as a reliable person, and that trust has been spurned. The dishonest statement is an insult and a hostile act. It is this aspect of the lie which Paul has in mind when he says – 'Putting away lying, speak every man truth with his neighbour: for we are members one of another' *(Ephesians 4.25)*.

The third alarming aspect of the lie is that the one who tells the lie is greatly injured by it. If adultery weakens the sinner, so does the lie. We cannot imagine how much we weaken ourselves when we lie. Just as freak waves may smash against a frail boat, fracturing the timbers, and eventually capsizing it, so each lie represents a shattering blow to the character. The next lie becomes much harder to resist, and soon the conscience is bludgeoned into insensitivity and personal integrity so impaired that the offender becomes a liar in character. Christ surely looks on, and says, 'That child of Mine no longer strives against sin; he is an habitual liar! That loved one for whom I suffered and died, that ambassador who represents Me in the world, has become a fallen, hopeless, compulsive liar!'

A further alarming aspect of the lie is the fact that every untruth is a multiple sin, and engenders other sins. There is usually a sinful motive for the lie, and yielding to it gives free rein to the sin behind it. Pride and arrogance, for example, are behind boastful lies; pride and cowardice behind dishonest excuses; and hatred, malice or jealousy behind vindictive gossip. Offences spawned by a lie include hypocrisy, because the liar tries to keep the appearance of being a Christian walking with the Lord and knowing His blessing.

The Devil's Campaign

The devil – who is the father of lies – is always trying to re-enslave believers in the habit of lying, often beginning his campaign with 'lesser' lies, such as exaggerations. He may put great pressure on us to exaggerate if only to get us accustomed to saying things which are not altogether true, and he scores a double victory if he can bring us to the point of even enjoying giving inflated or heavily garnished accounts of things. Some people lie and exaggerate to show off and attract attention to themselves. Others lie to win arguments, or to get favours. Sometimes people run down others in order to boost themselves by comparison. If our conscience smarts too much at uttering unkind lies about others, then Satan will introduce us to this practice in a gentle way, perhaps first tempting us only to retail the gossiping remarks of others. It may be that in time we will not worry so much about originating our own.

Another subtle introduction to the practice of lying is the defensive excuse or so-called 'white lie'. This is only a very little lie – Satan suggests to us – being told in a good cause. But inventive excuse-making is one of Satan's most effective ways of undermining a Christian's integrity. Let us suppose a believer has done something very foolish, or failed to do something important, and because the consequences will be embarrassing, he makes an excuse that bends the truth. His words are a lie, and so is his 'honest' stance and sincere facial expression. He has become an actor, and may, like an actor, tend to believe in the part he is playing. He may even feel wronged at having been challenged, and while he may know within himself that the excuse is false, he feels wholly justified in defending himself. The persistent maker of excuses becomes almost unaware that he is in the grip of a cowardly, defensive neurosis, as his conscience ceases to operate, and another hopeless liar grieves away the Spirit of God.

Sometimes the devil introduces a Christian to regular lying by first encouraging a flippant, loose spirit, with much 'light' talk, if possible about spiritual things. 'The Lord did this for me!' he says; 'The Lord sent me a bus;' 'The Lord told me not to go.' It is one thing to be grateful to God for all His provisions in daily life, but it is a foolish habit to ascribe all minor events to a direct, and special intervention of God, when we have no evidence for it. After all, God has determined that His people should prove Him while experiencing all the hardships as well as the benefits common to human society. The Lord certainly does intervene in our lives in a special way, in answer to prayer, but some Christians habitually claim such things. Do great claims to God's interventions glide off our lips easily, no matter how unreasonable? Flippant or glib speaking about the Lord's dealings with us is an apprenticeship in dishonesty. It is a subtle form of untruth. Remember that Satan is always trying to persuade us to play fast and loose with the truth; to be indifferent as to whether or not a thing *really* happened the way in which we have described it. We are being prepared like cattle for the slaughter, and even greater lies will soon follow.

Of course, in all that has just been said we would not want to banish colourful speech. There is a difference between the person who is gifted to give us a vivid description of something, and the person who is seriously exaggerating the facts. There are people whose descriptions are lively and enjoyable, throwing light on things that the rest of us do not readily see, but without dishonest distortion of the facts. They highlight aspects of situations – amusing ones perhaps – which may not occur to everyone. What we should avoid is exaggeration which stretches the truth by adding to or altering the facts, whether to deceive, or for a cheap laugh.

Unreliability and Pretence

Another subtle form of dishonesty which operates below the radar level of the conscience, but which Satan no doubt encourages to undermine integrity, is *unreliability*. This occurs in all areas of life, and also in the church. Perhaps someone is asked, 'Would you help in doing something for the Lord? Could you join in a workparty?'

'Oh yes,' comes the response, 'put my name down. I will come.' But this person does not turn up. Indeed, over the years it may be the case that this person hardly ever turns up. There is only a hairline's difference between unreliability and dishonesty. People who say they will do something when they have no intention of making sure they will do it, are not being truthful at all. They may not see themselves as liars, but they have developed the habit of taking no responsibility for their promises and commitments.

The withheld 'tithe' is a form of stealing from the Lord's work, and it is also an unspoken lie. In fact, it is a lie to the Holy Spirit, as we know from the case of Ananias and Sapphira. When we can afford our offering, and fail to give it, we lie to our fellow Christians, because we want to be thought of as dedicated believers, faithful to our Christian duties. In withholding our offerings we have a dark secret which we would not like to be known, but we are deceivers.

We mentioned earlier that lies do not have to be spoken. The writer remembers a young man (in the now distant past) who launched a dishonest set of allegations against others in his church, yet for months beforehand he had nothing but beaming smiles towards his victims. Though unspoken, his manner was an extreme form of deceit, and this kind of unspoken lie is frequently to be seen in the cordial greetings of people who need to be reconciled to each other. It is Satan's work.

What a terrible thing it is to have the conscience 'seared with a hot iron' as the result of 'speaking lies in hypocrisy' *(1 Timothy 4.2)*. The people to whom Paul refers were probably unconverted hypocrites, but his words are a solemn warning to us all. In this state the conscience no longer speaks when some false boast, exaggeration, invention or dishonest excuse crosses the tongue. The writer once knew a man whose deportment seemed to breathe integrity. Everyone who met him would have assumed he was a fine, old-fashioned gentleman in the best sense of the word, but the reality was that you never knew what devious, subtle deed this man would be up to next. Although dishonest, his measured, gentle manner had convinced him he was a model of integrity. If questioned about some underhanded scheme, it would always somehow be justified. Despite his bearing, he was sold under the power of the lie.

Are we pretenders? Do we engage in gushing, affected displays of cordiality or enthusiasm, not sincerely matched by what we think and feel? Are we phoney people? Do we put on airs and graces or project ourselves in a false way? Are we genuine in our motives and deeds? Are our plans really honest?

Let us keep our promises, avoiding like the plague deviousness, covering up and making false excuses, always remembering that the Lord abominates a lying tongue. Do we want to know the secret of drawing near to God in our devotions? Do we want a sense of the presence of the Lord? Let us begin by driving out lies and seeking truthfulness and genuineness of heart and mind. Only such a heart is a fit home for the Spirit of Truth.

Lies in the Lord's Work

We will not deal here with the incredible lies and exaggerations that characterise large sections of the charismatic constituency, because even in churches where truthfulness is desired and cherished, the temptation to lie is bound to be launched by the evil one. There is, for example, the form of dishonesty much exploited by Satan in bringing about the collapse of evangelical churches in the historic denominations in the 20th century. It is the make-believe or cover-up syndrome. When the writer was a teenager and not long converted, he was for a time in a Bible-believing church that was in such a denomination. This church's attitude to the denomination was of the make-believe type. In notices the church secretary would urge members to attend some meeting or other connected with 'our beloved denomination', the impression always being given that the denomination mirrored perfectly the biblical views of the congregation. The pastor spoke along the same lines, when the reality was that this church was one of a minority of evangelical congregations in a sea of liberal churches. The church leaders wanted to feel part of their denomination, and so looked at the denomination through rose-tinted spectacles, effectively concealing from members the

118 God's Rules for Holiness

shocking apostasy of that body. The pastor and officers flattered themselves that they were acting in love toward other churches, but in God's sight a form of deception was being carried on.

We see a similar attitude in 'house journals' published by large firms. They usually tell you what is good about the company, never what is bad. You would think you were in the most marvellous company to read the house journal, and not surprisingly, as it is produced by the public relations department. Unfortunately, the same kind of magazine misguidedly appears in church circles. A group of churches, perhaps good churches on the whole, decides to publish a periodical, an official organ for their group, reporting first on one church, then on another, emphasising the wonderful things undertaken and accomplished. Everything is perfect, and nothing is ever bad. When, sadly, a serious problem or error arises in the group, the house journal will hold its peace, because any comment would be negative, and possibly prove divisive.

The cry of the house journal is always – 'Pull together! Pull together!' – and never acknowledge that anything is wrong. But this is actually the sin of bearing false witness, and of crying, 'Peace, peace; when there is no peace' *(Jeremiah 6.14)*. It is injuring the people of God by treating the wounds of the churches as though they are not serious, and avoiding any ministry of warning. It is dishonest to convince the people that no heart-searching, review, repentance or repair is necessary, but this is the weakness of many groupings or associations even among fundamentally sound churches.

Ministers and office bearers are not immune from the creeping poison of dishonesty, especially as the need for diplomacy and discretion in their work leads all too easily to the use of half-truths and concealment. However, there are matters which people are entitled to know about. In the last day, when all hidden things shall be known, it may be revealed that many churches lost their blessing and usefulness because the Spirit of God was offended by under-handedness. At an individual level, does a preacher present anecdotes as true, when they never really happened? Men who do this foolishly undermine their integrity, and will soon lie about any-thing.

Hypocrisy has been defined as wickedness paying homage to righteousness, and yet it is more, because it involves dishonest pre-tence, making it a lie. Years ago there was a preacher well respected among the churches of his county, but a source of perplexity to some of his own congregation, who, as they called at his house, over a number of years, would hear his voice raised in terrible abuse towards his wife. He apparently did little to control his temper, but he serenely continued with his pulpit ministry as though the unc-tion of God would never be denied him. His unbridled but (so he thought) concealed sin made him a hypocrite and a liar. Will the final day show that the lack of spiritual fruit in many a church was due, not to the coldness of the neighbourhood or any of the other often-heard reasons, but to a lack of integrity somewhere in the leadership of the church? How many Achanite sins will be revealed in the last day?

All troubles in a church involve false witness at some point. Some-times good people fall by degrees into a state of contention because they underestimate the power of dishonesty. They feel strongly about something, and they may well be right, but instead of raising the problem in the right quarter they smoulder on it, murmuring in the shadows. Meanwhile they continue to behave towards the church leaders as though they are perfectly happy about everything. Soon they find it difficult to either raise their complaint in a right spirit or to trust anyone to respond to them. Gradually, bitterness and resentment sets in and they proceed to complain more openly about almost everything.

In relating this litany of troubles, we do not want to give the impression that these are typical of evangelical churches, for it is this writer's testimony that believers are the very best of people in this dark world, and he is constantly moved to admire the gracious and godly spirit of so very many of them. Their lives show the goodness and power of the Lord, and there is nothing to be compared with them in the world of unbelievers.

But how long does it take for the devil to turn a well-meaning Christian into an injurious liar? We can only exhort ourselves to flee from every form of hypocrisy and deceit. We must be afraid of being snared by such things, and we must value and keep tight hold on the spirit of truthfulness. The devil can turn us so easily – if we let him – into people who smile charmingly one minute, and are hostile and bitter the next. How disappointing it is to have Christians in a church whose real heart you can never be sure of! We must be genuine people, for – 'the wisdom that is from above is first pure, then peaceable, gentle, and easy to be intreated, full of mercy and good fruits, without partiality, and without hypocrisy' *(James 3.17).*

Defeating the Lie

Truthfulness is so precious to God and so vital to our spiritual good that the campaign against a lying tongue must never be relaxed. As we pray, the Holy Spirit of God will activate our conscience, making it very sensitive to any rising lie, and we will find ourselves on the alert and ready for the inventions of 'the flesh'. Should our own fallen heart, or Satan, propose a lie, as soon as the residual sin-nature begins to nurture it, then the conscience will throw us into discomfort and we shall prove the truth of Paul's words – 'For the flesh lusteth against the Spirit, and the Spirit against the flesh: and these are contrary the one to the other: so that ye cannot do the things that ye *[otherwise]* would' *(Galatians 5.17).* The barb or prick of conscience is the time to stop the lie and to pray for power over the tongue, and if this is done, then the Holy Spirit helps, the temptation to sin is defeated, and the implicit promise of *Galatians 5.16* fulfilled – 'Walk in the Spirit, and ye shall not fulfil the lust of the flesh.'

If, however, we proceed to utter the lie (or participate in the hearing of the lying gossip), then we sin against the alerting, restraining work of the Spirit through the conscience, abusing not only the standard but also the help of God, and if we do this repeatedly, we should not be surprised that the Spirit is grieved away, and the conscience rendered inactive. When a believer becomes conscious of having lied only after the lie has been uttered, it is a sign that the voice of conscience has been trampled over too often and is no longer giving advance warning. Says the psalmist – 'To day if ye will hear his voice, harden not your heart.' We must always pray for tender consciences, and when God the Holy Spirit answers our cry, we must treasure and value His gift, heeding every warning, and co-operating fully. This is the only way we can keep the commandment – 'Thou shalt not bear false witness.'

10

The Tenth Commandment
'Thou shalt not covet.'

Enemy of the Heart

> 'Let your conversation be without covetousness;
> and be content with such things as ye have: for he hath said,
> I will never leave thee, nor forsake thee.'
>
> *(Hebrews 13.5)*

HOW GOD'S WORD analyses us! There is no work in secular literature which so lays bare the deep flaws of the heart, and traces the 'root' sins of the human condition. We have already observed that these commandments must be couched in negative terms because we are a race in rebellion against God, and they must set out the basis of judgement, and stir us to see our need of grace. However, we must also search out the opposite, positive virtues which in the case of the tenth commandment are – contentedness, reasonableness, modesty and self-control. Viewed another way, covetousness is a craving for *personal* and *earthly* benefits, and so the opposite quality is the cultivation of a heart occupied by the Lord's interests, and the needs of others.

To covet is to crave for things, setting the heart upon them. The human mind is full of dreams, schemes and fancies, which are the 'props' people depend upon to be happy and to keep going in life. If they cannot fix their minds on desirable things they become miserable and unmotivated. Coveting is the mainspring of life for our rebellious race. The tenth commandment covers both the determined pursuit of a desired object, and also the underdog form of coveting, which is envy and jealousy of others who have greater possessions and advantages in life.*

Coveting is the act of focusing the mind on such things as property, possessions, success, esteem, status, fame, popularity, position, and personal appearance, or on expressly forbidden goals such as 'thy neighbour's wife'. The former things are not morally forbidden, but covetousness dedicates the heart to dreaming and scheming for the things that belong down here, in this life, in this present world, and depending on them for some degree of happiness and fulfilment. All this is deeply offensive to the Lord Who made us to be the highest of His creatures, and Who gave us the power to know Him. In covetousness, He sees us grovelling for satisfaction in the material realm; hungering and thirsting only for things to do with the body – money, clothing, superior home, fancy car, prestigious job, expensive objects, and so many other things beside. As for the Lord, He is effectively put in second place as a source of satisfaction and succour. We say we love Him, but not enough to be fulfilled and satisfied by Him.

---

* In the New Testament the sin of covetousness is described by various Greek words, which mean – to passionately set the heart upon some objective, or to want more, to be eager for gain; to be a lover of silver; or to stretch and reach out for something. References to *lust* in the New Testament frequently refer to covetous behaviour.

Eight Effects of Covetousness
1. It takes over the heart

Covetousness is particularly offensive to God because it takes over the heart, pushing out higher desires and emotions. Covetousness is like floodwater from a river which has burst its banks, the swirling torrent knowing no direction or self-control. It does not make a detour round a beautiful garden in order that it may be preserved, but is ruthless and undiscriminating in its rush to cover the ground. Dreaming after material things leads to the heart being quickly over-run by imagined need, greed and desire. Soon the things of God are no longer enjoyable, and the spirit of sacrifice and service is quenched.

In the parable of the sower the Lord speaks of those who are choked with the cares, riches and pleasures of this life, cut off from the Word of God, and unable to manifest spiritual conviction and fruit. It is possible for people to be so affected by the Gospel that they feel very deeply the vanity of life without God and the need of His mercy and forgiveness, yet the 'thorns' of covetousness can choke these feelings within hours.

For believers also, covetousness can sweep away all spiritual interest, proving the Lord's words – 'Ye cannot serve God and mammon.' Any Christian who thinks that the desire for possessions, fame, popularity, admiration, worldly success, comfort and excessive earthly pleasure can be kept in bounds has not learned the most basic lesson of human nature – mammon always takes over. We have only to carry out the briefest survey of our own experience to see how true this is. As soon as we give over our minds and imagination to dreaming about material objectives, spiritual matters instantly become less interesting. All the enthusiasm and emotional energy which is needed to drive the truly important spiritual activities of our lives, evaporates.

2. It both weakens and coarsens

Covetousness is like an aggressive form of cancer, rapidly overwhelming its victim, or a potentially fatal virus attacking someone who is fit and strong. Even worse, covetousness not only weakens, it also coarsens, as the tenth commandment shows. Notice how the commandment is expressed: 'Thou shalt not covet thy neighbour's wife.' Here is a two-fold indictment, namely that covetousness will not hesitate to deprive another person, but will also smash through the seventh commandment, if it feels the desire. The covetous person, under the power of 'wanting', may be reduced to the gross insensitivity and moral indifference of wife stealing. Once we begin to covet, then even colleagues, acquaintances, friends or relatives may become the object of our jealousy and resentment, to the extent that, given the chance, we would take whatever we wanted from them.

Covetousness takes the believer's eyes away from the well-being of the 'neighbour' and focuses them on that neighbour's possessions and advantages. Once coarsened by a covetous attitude, the capacity for true friendship and unselfish affection is seriously impaired, because everyone represents a challenge and an object of comparison. The believer can no longer relate to others without noticing their homes, possessions, incomes, and opportunities. 'Are we not at least as good as they are?' asks the heart. 'Why should they be so much better off in various ways?'

3. It is an act of worship

God hates covetousness because it so diminishes people – even *His* people. It makes a believer a domestic creature; a pathetic, little being in His sight. Made in God's image, we reduce ourselves to the lowest level of life, shutting out the higher, spiritual purposes, motivated chiefly by earthly, fleeting things, and preoccupied with the trivial. As we should expect, the Lord particularly hates covetousness because it is an act of worship – an appropriate term for the powerful longings for material things that involves a kind of dependence of soul, as though we would be miserable without them. Hours of mental planning are devoted to the achievement of material goals and possessions, and when finally secured, these are cherished, exhibited, and jealously protected.

4. It is infectious

Another aspect of covetousness to be feared is its infectious nature. It probably ranks equal with gossiping as the most infectious of church-hurting sins. Once self-pampering and delight in unnecessarily expensive or elaborate possessions takes up an acceptable place in a church fellowship, it rapidly undermines wholehearted commitment and realistic stewardship. Those who are young in the faith observe the dependence upon earthly comforts and luxuries characterising more mature believers, and their consciences are quickly defiled. The destructive power of example is nowhere more noticed than in the covetousness of many Christians.

Covetousness is undoubtedly rated in the New Testament as being equal to idolatry, but in modern evangelicalism it is scarcely regarded as sinful at all. Sometimes the man with the most luxurious house and car is the very first to be thought of as suitable for eldership. Supposedly Christian people in public life or the world of entertainment ostentatiously display their fabulously rich, worldly lifestyles without forfeiting any of the applause they get from many Christian magazines.

5. It is addictive and progressive

A further reason for fearing covetousness is that it is powerfully addictive and progressive. The devil puts into the mind of a believer the idea that a certain possession or position will bring great satisfaction, and consequently, much time and energy is dedicated to obtaining it. The desired goal becomes a motivating force and a chief topic of thoughts and dreams. In due course the goal will be achieved, but all too soon the heart grows used to it, and dissatisfaction and emptiness set in again. The only way out is to fix upon another promising, alluring goal to provide inspiration and motivation, and a constantly recurring addictive cycle is established. The believer is now at the mercy of appetites like a cork bobbing about on the sea, driven along by countless foolish and hurtful lusts which can never be satisfied for long.

6. It is an 'invisible' sin

Above all, covetousness is the prince of *invisible* sins – invisible, that is, to the offender. When, in *Romans 7.7*, Paul argues that without the law we would be unaware of the extent of our sin, he selects covetousness as the outstanding example of 'self-concealment'. He writes: 'For I had not known lust, except the law had said, Thou shalt not covet.' Here, then, is the chief example of an *invisible* sin; a sin that has the capacity to so disguise itself that the offender is barely conscious of his trangression. Part of the reason for this is the fact that covetousness is the most self-justifying sin, for we expertly construct a reasonable case for whatever we want. Surely it is very *useful*. Furthermore it is very *necessary*. It will be good for witness, and it is a bargain. In no time a luxury becomes a necessity. Covetousness is a highly subtle sin, which anaesthetises and extinguishes the conscience by its very process of action.

7. It is a root of apostasy

We learn from *2 Timothy 3.1-2* that – 'In the last days perilous times shall come. For men shall be lovers of their own selves, covetous . . . ' Out of thirteen evil characteristics of an apostate society, listed by Paul, the second is the sin of covetousness. We certainly live now in doctrinally perilous or dangerous times when many who claim to be Bible believers are throwing aside the old standards of the faith and compromising with worldliness and error. How do we account for the blatant weakness of so many evangelical leaders who have sold the pass to worldly music and methods in church life? At the top of Paul's list are self-consideration and covetousness.

Once leaders begin to be concerned about their security, acceptability, advancement, well-being and possessions they will cease to stand firmly for the standards of the Word, stressing diplomacy above faithfulness, peace in preference to purity, and diversity over God's narrow road. The moment God's servant indulges covetous desires for comfort, security, position or possessions, these things will rapidly assume such importance that he will abandon the defence of the old ways, and then one disloyalty will lead to another as he adjusts his views to get or to keep his material benefits. This is the trap into which Satan has brought many an unguarded leader through the long history of Gospel churches. If we are unfaithful in the material things of life – mammon – we shall certainly prove disloyal with the true riches. In *1 Timothy 3.3* Paul directs that a man should never be appointed as an elder (which includes a preacher) if he is covetous, and the same standard is then applied to deacons. Church leaders must be content with their lot. They must be people who have an eye for the needs and difficulties of others, not for themselves and their material gain.

The relationship between covetous desire and doctrinal collapse on the part of the congregation is brought out in *2 Timothy 4.3-4*, where Paul says: 'For the time will come when they will not endure sound doctrine; but after their own LUSTS shall they heap to themselves teachers . . . and they shall turn away their ears from the truth.' The word here translated *lusts* means – longings or strong desires. The verse suggests that congregations will call the kind of pastor who will allow them to do and have what they want – men who will seldom exhort, admonish or challenge them about their excessive and comfortable lifestyle. We see this in many churches today, where people are allowed to live in a self-seeking, leisure-loving, worldly way, and at the same time are flattered from the pulpit into thinking they are still loyal disciples of Christ. Such people cannot stand *sound* teaching, which includes all the counsel of God and which searches the *heart* and *conduct* of believers, so they select preachers who will never challenge their sin. This is becoming a guaranteed way of building a reasonably large congregation in many parts of the world. Preach the theoretical doctrines of the Bible – even the glorious doctrines of grace – so as to stretch and flatter the intellects of the hearers, but take care *never* to rebuke covetousness, in any of its manifestations.

8. It may lead to 'excommunication'

The seriousness of covetousness is seen from many strong warnings, such as *1 Corinthians 5.11* where Paul says that it may warrant excommincation from the churches of Christ. He writes: 'But now I have written unto you not to keep company, if any man that is called a brother be a fornicator, OR COVETOUS, or an idolater, or a railer, or a drunkard, or an extortioner; with such an one no not to eat.' The Greek word here refers to someone who is eager for gain; always wanting more. It may be a craving for money and possessions, or it may be a desire for position, influence or recognition. Obviously the Scripture has in mind a serious and persistent state for the serious discipline prescribed.

In *1 Corinthians 6.10* Paul reinforces the case in these words: 'Nor thieves, NOR COVETOUS, nor drunkards, nor revilers, nor extortioners, shall inherit the kingdom of God.' A similar warning is repeated in *Ephesians 5.5* where we are bluntly told that a covetous man is an idolater, who has no place in the kingdom of Christ. Perhaps we need to be frightened out of our covetousness.

We see the need for putting an offender out of fellowship in a serious case from the words of Paul in *1 Timothy 6.9-10*: 'They that will be rich fall into temptation and a snare, and into many foolish and hurtful lusts, which drown men in destruction and perdition. For the love of money is the root of all evil: which while some coveted after, they have erred from the faith, and pierced themselves through with many sorrows.'

How to Avoid Covetousness

1. Keeping spiritual priorities

How is covetousness to be avoided? A great lesson may be learned from the behaviour of the children of Israel in the wilderness, of whom Paul says: 'Now these things were our examples, to the intent we should not lust after evil things, as they also lusted' *(1 Corinthians 10.6)*. He refers to an event recorded in *Numbers 11.4,* when the children of Israel found God's manna distasteful and spoke disdainfully of it. Their hearts began to lust after such apparently innocent things as fish, cucumbers, melons, leeks, onions and garlic. God was not angry with them because those foods were evil, but because they wanted them so much that they wished they could be back in Egypt. Even worse, they wanted them more than the manna which God had given them. Instead of being grateful, and saying, 'God is clearly with us, taking us to a better land,' they murmured with discontent, and longed for material benefits.

Anything which is desired more than the spiritual blessing of God is, for the believer, an evil thing. The highway to covetousness is to lose appreciation of what He has provided for us. The moment we begin to take our blessings for granted, we begin to need the 'melons' and 'cucumbers' of this vain world. The first safeguard, therefore, against the virus of covetousness is to have a truly thankful spirit, full of genuine gratitude and praise to God. We need to review frequently His mercy and goodness, meaning with all our hearts the hymns of praise which we sing, and acknowledging that we are not worthy of the least of all His mercies. We need to marvel and rejoice in the great privileges of the Christian life, taking special steps to recall these things in times of trial, disappointment or depression.

2. Walking in the Spirit

Another antidote to covetousness is given to us in *Galatians 5.16* – 'This I say then, Walk in the Spirit, and ye shall not fulfil the lust of the flesh.' Walking in the Spirit, the Christian receives all the help that is needed to stop the desires of the heart from going after worldly and selfish things. He prays for help regularly, co-operating with the Holy Spirit's work in the conscience. Whenever the Spirit activates a pang of conscience because the believer begins to desire strongly some worldly gain or advancement, he promptly responds. If the believer then draws back from that extravagant purchase or ambitious pursuit, then a victory is won, but if the Spirit's gracious ministry is brushed aside, the sin of covetousness will follow.

Walking in the Spirit includes putting spiritual service first in life. If a believer has no avenue of service for the Lord, no sacrifice, no commitment, then it is too easy for that believer's emotional energy to be poured into personal needs and aspirations. Such a Christian will become easy prey to covetous desire. Those who are totally devoted to home or career have a hard time fighting the lusts of the flesh, because they are not really walking in the Spirit. They are less concerned about His work and kingdom than about their own affairs, and so they will always be at the mercy of their fallen hearts.

3. Mortifying covetous desires

The greatest weapon against covetousness, mentioned in so many texts, is that of active resistance to it. Mortification, or putting covetousness to death, cannot be skipped. The moment we stop fighting against the many subtle temptations to covet this or that, we slide away from the right path. In *Galatians 5.24* Paul defines Christians as those who have – 'crucified the flesh with the affections and lusts'. Once again, the word *lusts* refers to longings, desires, and affection for earthly things as well as immoral thoughts.

Ephesians 4.22 tells us to 'put off . . . the old man, which is corrupt according to the deceitful lusts.' The old nature within us would love to dominate once again, and to bring us under the rule of our earthly appetites, but we must resist these drawings, never for a moment giving way to them. The old nature is very crafty, and, aided and abetted by the devil's suggestions, it will keep up a relentless campaign to rekindle our love of the things of this vain world. There will be times of tranquillity, when we shall enjoy great contentment with our lot in life and love our spiritual blessings and privileges best, and then, suddenly perhaps, a great assault of temptations to envy, self-pity, and desire will be launched upon us. We must be conscious of our vulnerability, and always be ready to deny ourselves the unnecessary acquisition, the superfluous possession, or the unjustifiable extra quality or price-tag.

When Paul says to Timothy, 'Flee also youthful lusts' *(2 Timothy 2.22)*, it is often assumed that he refers to sexual urges. But the Greek word for *lusts* is the word for longings and desires which covers any or all human appetites, and which equally applies to covetousness. The lusts which Paul has in mind are particularly strong in the young, and might well include sinful sexual desires, but 'youthful lusts' equally includes ambition and possessions. Ambition becomes covetous when we long for something for *ourselves*; for personal gratification, and for gain.

In effect Paul says, 'When day-dreams begin, in which you are at the centre of the stage, with people admiring you and your gifts, then flee from those thoughts. Transfer your thinking to something else. Run, as if running from an impending catastrophe.'

4. Controlling the thought life

To resist covetousness we need to *do* something about controlling our thought life. Dreams and desires are not meant to go unchecked and uncontrolled. The command of Scripture is – 'Let not sin therefore reign in your mortal body, that ye should obey it in the lusts *[lit: longings and desires]* thereof' *(Romans 6.12)*. Therefore, when self-promoting thoughts come into the head, we must not abandon our defences and allow them to develop and reign. God's command to us is – Stop scheming! Stop dreaming! Direct the imagination to better things. Recognise the wiles of Satan in these thoughts. If necessary, and especially if temptations to be, or to buy, or to possess, are coming thick and fast, keep nearby some activity or book which never fails to absorb you, so that you can more easily win the battle of expelling these unwanted urges.

The biblical method of dealing with covetousness is to put up a tremendous fight against it. We must absolutely refuse to give in to our desires for things which we do not really need, or which are far beyond the price and quality which is reasonably appropriate. Of course, always we must pray for help, and we shall receive it. And always we must avoid things which have the effect of stirring up covetous thoughts – such as the opulent homes of some worldly, covetous 'Christians', or catalogues filled with desirable wares.

It is in the context of speaking about the Commandments (including 'Thou shalt not covet') that Paul says in *Romans 13.14* – 'But put ye on the Lord Jesus Christ, and make not provision *[lit: forethought]* for the flesh, to fulfil the lusts thereof.' We may paraphrase this verse thus: 'Do not think ahead or make plans about matters which only pander to your carnal longings and desires, and which will enable those lusts to be fulfilled.' Truly, the world of daydreams is the birthplace and cradle of covetous sins.

The Rewards of Reasonableness

On a positive note, the work of resisting covetousness carries great rewards for believers, even during this earthly life. Indeed, all the promises of God for our present spiritual happiness are dependent on our standing clear from covetousness, as we learn in *2 Peter 1.4:* 'Whereby are given unto us exceeding great and precious promises: that by these ye might be partakers of the divine nature, having escaped the corruption that is in the world through lust.'

Do we escape that corruption? Are we pleasing to God? Can we receive the fruit of His great and precious promises to make Himself known to us, to open the eyes of our understanding, to grant us a great sense of belonging, and to privilege us with growth in grace and instrumentality in the bringing in of His elect people?

Let us take no notice of those Christian believers who make a pact with this world, indulging their desires and acquiring whatever they want. Ambitious and self-seeking believers, whether in secular professions or in the ministry, must be seen as tragedies, not as models for other believers. Remember the word of Christ – 'They have their reward' *(Matthew 6.2, 5, 16)*. What blessings will be ours, if only we put up a great fight against fleshly covetousness, praying for the Spirit to help us.

The 'Secret' of Blessing

'But now being made free from sin,
and become servants to God, ye have your
fruit unto holiness . . .'
(Romans 6.22)

THERE IS A common tendency in human thinking to seek one major point or principle that will solve everything and prove to be the 'secret' of success. This tendency is found in Christian circles also, and some preachers and writers, past and present, have claimed to have found the great central issue that leads to continuous joy and spiritual fruitfulness. Various 'secrets' have been advanced, such as the 'higher life' idea of sanctification by faith, the so-called gifts of the Spirit, and more recently 'delighting in God' as the key driving principle of the Christian life. However, it is never wise to make any one thing, even a wholesome practice, the single or chief pathway to blessing. Christ is the key to everything for believers, to know Him, to have Him, to love Him, to serve Him, and to look forward to being with Him, and Christ has given us a multiplicity of 'goals' in the great summary of the law – 'Thou shalt love the Lord thy God with all thy heart, and with all thy soul, and with all thy strength, and with all thy mind; and thy neighbour as thyself' *(Luke 10.27).*

If, following conversion to Christ by grace alone, we allow the standards of the moral law to search our hearts, inspire our souls, direct our strength and rule our minds, then we truly set foot on the highway of sanctification, in dependence on the help of the Holy Spirit. The moral law continues as our standard, guide and protection. Even distinctively spiritual duties such as faith, love and sincerity are in the moral law, especially in the first two commandments which are all about loving God and trusting Him alone, the third emphasising sincerity.

To saved eyes, nearly every right and spiritual disposition of heart is here. Certainly, there are also Gospel duties – such as witness to Christ – which are distinctively found in the New Testament, but the Commandments provide a grand and vital survey of holiness, when rightly understood.

How much we need holiness! There can be no real expression of love for Christ without it, for He said – 'If ye love me, keep my commandments' *(John 14.15).* Nor can there be great assurance, because John said, 'Let us not love in word, neither in tongue; but in deed and in truth. And hereby we know that we are of the truth, and shall assure our hearts before him' *(1 John 3.18-19).* Instrumentality in personal witness and church growth also depends on holy living, for Paul said, 'Let every one that nameth the name of Christ depart from iniquity' in order to be 'sanctified, and meet for the master's use' *(2 Timothy 2.19-21).* Truly effective prayer equally needs holiness, for James said, 'The effectual fervent prayer of a righteous man availeth much' *(James 5.16).* Strength in times of trial also comes from holiness, as we learn from Peter, who, when speaking about how to handle troubles, gives this 'method' as a crowning exhortation: 'So be ye holy in all manner of conversation' (see *1 Peter 1.6-15).*

Who, then, dare single out any one spiritual duty as the means of succeeding in every other obligation? The Lord gives us whole families of sins to avoid, and qualities to embrace in the divinely deep code of the Ten Commandments – 'That the man of God may be perfect, throughly furnished unto all good works.' Our chief motive for the pursuit of holiness must be the sentiment expressed by Isaac Watts –

Love so amazing, so divine,
Demands my life, my soul, my all.

'The law of the Lord is perfect, converting the soul:
the testimony of the Lord is sure, making wise the simple.
The statutes of the Lord are right, rejoicing the heart:
the commandment of the Lord is pure, enlightening the eyes.
The fear of the Lord is clean, enduring for ever:
the judgments of the Lord are true and righteous altogether.
More to be desired are they than gold, yea, than much fine gold:
sweeter also than honey and the honeycomb.
Moreover by them is thy servant warned: and in keeping of
them there is great reward'
(Psalm 19.7-11).

Verses Confirming the Abiding Authority of the Commandments

Jeremiah 31.31-33 and *Hebrews 10.15-16*: Through Jeremiah, God declares that when the New Testament age comes, church members will have 'my law' (ie: His unchanging law) written in their hearts in a special way.

Romans 3.20: God's Commandments define sin. If they change, or some cease to apply, then sin also changes.

Romans 7.12 and *14*: Paul affirms that the moral law is – holy, and just, and good. It is spiritual, which means that it is the work of the Holy Spirit and that it reflects the unchanging character of God.

Romans 13.8-10: Paul shows saved people that they should strive to fulfil the ancient Commandments.

James 2.8, 11 and *12*: James requires obedience to the moral law, but shows that for saved people it is not a law of condemnation (for they have received the royal pardon) but a law of liberty. As free people they willingly obey their King's Commandments.

1 John 3.4: The law continues as the sole and abiding standard of righteousness.

1 John 5.2-3: The ultimate mark of true conversion is that we love God and obey the Ten Commandments. Furthermore, we do not feel aggrieved or annoyed by them, but value them as the standards and counsel of God.

Worship in the Melting Pot

Peter Masters

148 pages, paperback, ISBN 1 870855 33 7

'Worship is truly in the melting pot,' says the author. 'A new style of praise has swept into evangelical life shaking to the foundations traditional concepts and attitudes.' How should we react? Is it all just a matter of taste and age? Will churches be helped, or changed beyond recognition?

This book presents four essential principles which Jesus Christ laid down for worship, and by which every new idea must be judged.

Here also is a fascinating view of how they worshipped in Bible times, including their rules for the use of instruments, and the question is answered – What does the Bible teach about the content and order of a service of worship today?

Physicians of Souls

The Gospel Ministry

Peter Masters

285 pages, paperback, ISBN 1 870855 34 5

'Compelling, convicting, persuasive preaching, revealing God's mercy and redemption to dying souls, is seldom heard today. The noblest art ever granted to our fallen human race has almost disappeared.'

Even where the free offer of the Gospel is treasured in principle, regular evangelistic preaching has become a rarity, contends the author. These pages tackle the inhibitions, theological and practical, and provide powerful encouragement for physicians of souls to preach the Gospel. A vital anatomy or order of conversion is supplied with advice for counselling seekers.

The author shows how passages for evangelistic persuasion may be selected and prepared. He also challenges modern church growth techniques, showing the superiority of direct proclamation. These and other key topics make up a complete guide to soulwinning.

The Lord's Pattern for Prayer

Peter Masters

118 pages, paperback, ISBN 1 870855 36 1

Studying the lessons and spiritual encouragements in the most famous of prayers. This volume is almost a manual on prayer, providing a real spur to the devotional life. The Lord's own plan and agenda for prayer – carefully amplified – takes us into the presence of the Father, to prove the privileges and power of God's promises to those who pray.

Chapters cover each petition of the Lord's Prayer. Here, too, are sections on remedies for problems in prayer, how to intercede for others, the reasons why God keeps us waiting for answers, and the nature of the prayer of faith.

Do We Have a Policy?

For Church Health and Growth

93 pages, paperback, ISBN 1 870855 30 2

Biblical Strategies for Witness

154 pages, paperback, ISBN 1 870855 18 3

Steps for Guidance

184 pages, paperback, ISBN 1 870855 19 1

Only One Baptism of the Holy Spirit

109 pages, paperback, ISBN 1 870855 17 5

The Charismatic Phenomenon [co-authored with John C. Whitcomb]

113 pages, paperback, ISBN 1 870855 01 9

The Healing Epidemic

227 pages, paperback, ISBN 1 870855 00 0

Should Christians Drink?

The Case for Total Abstinence

110 pages, paperback, ISBN 1 870855 12 4

www.wakemantrust.org